One Flesh Revolution

Start, Strengthen And *Sustain* Marital Oneness

By Seth Widner

The purpose for this book is to benefit marriages and families. If you would like to request permission to use this book for benefitting marriages and families, contact Seth Widner. He would love to hear from you.

All Scripture quotations are taken from the HOLY BIBLE, NEW INTERNATIONAL VERSION ®. Copyright © 1973, 1978, 1984 by International Bible Society. Used by permission of Zondervan. All rights reserved.

The Absent Father and Overly Bonded With Mother Wounds in Chapter 3 "Aftermath: Our Wounded Generation" came from Mens Fraternity: The Quest For Authentic Manhood written by Robert Lewis. Robert Lewis gave Seth Widner permission. For more information about Mens Fraternity or 33 Series, visit www.mensfraternity.com or
www.33theseries.com

Cover Design by Brandon Harless.

Photo on the book back by Brandon Scott Beavers.

ISBN 978-1481055154

Contents

For Jesus Christ, the One who provides the opportunity for us to live as one flesh. You empower us by Your Spirit. You lead us by the truth in Your Word. And Your grace is sufficient.

Dedicated to my Melissa Queen. When my knee dropped on that wooden ground in the summer of long ago, You said yes! You have quenched my thirst for respect from the well of Your heart. I will continue to cherish You until I breathe my last. And when that day comes, we will still be holding hands.

Forward

Wow, can I get a GO GOD on the book One Flesh Revolution! Thank you Seth for your off the charts biblical insight to what God's design for a covenant marriage looks like. No doubt this book points all couples whether engaged, newlywed, or old veterans how to maintain a healthy marriage and remain one flesh.

–Darryl Bellar

Lead Pastor of the Journey Church

www.thejourneyfamily.com

Introduction

There are few things better than a fresh cup of coffee in the morning. Like most people, I like mine a particular way. After filling the cup two-thirds full, it is time to add some flavor. So I begin with some sugar. After sprinkling some sugar into my cup, I add a little more. You can never have too much of a good thing! Then I add two hazel nut creamers. Notice that I said hazel nut creamers. Through countless morning rituals, I have found this flavor to be the best. As I stir up my cup of goodness, all the ingredients become one.

Now that my cup of coffee is prepared, I patiently wait for that first sip. Timing is everything. If I rush it, my lips will pay the price. So I carry it to my office and set the cup next to my computer. As I wait for the perfect moment, I glance at my calendar and prepare for the day's tasks. The fresh aroma fills my office and gives me something to look forward to.

When the timing is right, I gently pick up the cup of coffee. As I bring it close to my face, I breathe in the aroma deeply. *Oh yes, this first sip is going to be amazing.* Then I enjoy that first sip. The flavor flows over my taste buds and fills my body with a warm sensation. This is the perfect way to start any day! I am now prepared to handle anything that life may throw my way.

On one particular morning, I prepared my cup of coffee and laid it on my desk. As it cooled off, I began to tackle some daily tasks. One of these tasks involved an errand. As I re-entered my office, I reached for the cup of coffee. Just like most mornings, I was looking forward to the first sip of the day. As the coffee flowed over my taste buds, I quickly spit it back into the cup. *Yuck!!! Disgusting!!!* Apparently, I had made a mistake. What happened? I grabbed the wrong cup. Instead of picking up my fresh cup of coffee, I selected yesterday's cup. Not the same!

At first glance, both cups of coffee looked the same. Each cup contained the same ingredients of coffee, sugar and hazel nut cream. Although both cups were similar, they held a tremendous difference. One cup was warm and the other was cold.

Now the warm cup of coffee would represent a real deal marriage. This is what we all hope to gain. What does a real-deal marriage look like? What does it entail? Is your marriage the real deal? Or could you be settling for something less? Deep down, you know the answer to these questions. And based on my experience of ministering to husbands and wives, many couples are faking it instead of making it. If this describes your marriage, you are not alone. And change is within your reach. You do not have to fake it. You can actually make it!

The purpose for this book is to show you God's design for marriage. For it is the real deal. I want to personally invite you to examine the real deal with me. By doing so, your eyes will see the way marriage is supposed to be. And you will be equipped to experience God's best with your spouse.

My wife, Melissa, recently attended the wedding of a close friend. Since I was traveling at the time, I couldn't attend the wedding with her. During the reception, Melissa called me. She asked me to offer some marriage advice to our newly-wed friends. I paused to think of what to say. *What advice should I give them? What insight should I provide concerning one of God's greatest gifts?* My mind was filled with all kinds of possibilities. But I knew that my friends did not have the time to listen to all of my thoughts. They had a honeymoon to enjoy!

So I offered this piece of advice. *Never think you've arrived.* Always seek to grow in your God-given role as husband or wife. Understand that you will never know it all. Why? Marriage is such a deep relationship! Through marriage, two totally separate people become one flesh. The marriage relationship involves unpredictable seasons and an array of emotions. Living as one flesh can be simple or complex, sometimes both at the same time! Husbands and wives become life-long students to God's intricate design for marriage.

I do not claim to be a know-it-all concerning marriage. God has not bestowed all marital knowledge to me. I am just an ordinary guy who still has plenty of room to learn and grow. I'm sure there are more qualified authors who have the ability to write in-depth material for husbands and wives. So why am I writing this book?

Although I'm an ordinary guy, God has me on an extraordinary mission. I'm helping husbands and wives experience God's best. Our culture is flooded with countless theories concerning marriage. In fact, some theories even question the need for marriage! One expert says to do this and another says to do that. And you will rarely find two experts who agree with one another. This world of contradicting experts is causing a lot of confusion. It seems that couples are frantically seeking new knowledge for experiencing a healthy marriage. Why? They are looking for something that works.

The answers that we seek cannot be found in brand new ideas. The path to a healthy marriage can be found through the ancient principles of God's Word. Instead of chasing after every new idea that is introduced to society, we need to return to God's original design. Although I am not an expert, I do understand God's design! I have also learned, through observation and experience, that God's design works. And I want to share it with you. Through this book, you will learn how to start, strengthen and sustain a healthy marriage. God wants you to be one with your spouse.

- *Start* living out God's wonderful design for your marriage!

- *Strengthen* your relationship with your spouse!

- *Sustain* ongoing oneness through all seasons of life!

I believe that it is time for a revolution! God's design for marriage works. It is time for husbands and wives to stop living a counterfeit existence. We must stop settling for false illusions of a healthy marriage. It is time for husbands and wives to experience the real deal. Your marriage matters. My marriage matters. Our families matter! We must turn away from the confusion of our society and take hold of principles that are proven true. Let's chase after God's best together. Are you with me? Let the One Flesh Revolution begin!

God's Promise

"Blessed is the man who does not walk in the counsel of the wicked or stand in the way of sinners or sit in the seat of mockers. But his delight is in the law of the LORD and on his law he meditates day and night. He is like a tree planted by streams of water, which yields its fruit in season and whose leaf does not wither. Whatever he does prospers." - Psalm 1:1-3

When Melissa and I were newly weds, we lived in Lenoir City, Tennessee. One morning, Melissa discovered that her car would not start. She came back into our townhouse and told me. So I went outside to look over the situation. I put the key in the ignition and tried to start the engine. Nothing happened. *The battery must be dead,* I thought to myself. The reason I suspected a dead battery is because that is one of the few things I can fix on a car. Other than a basic oil or battery change, I'm useless as a car mechanic. In fact, if my profession were auto repair, my family would starve!

I quickly popped the hood and looked for the car battery. After a quick glance to the left and right, I didn't see the battery. So I took a second look. I still did not see it. At this point, I was becoming embarrassed. *How hard can it be to locate a car battery? What will I say to Melissa? Hey Babe, I failed the simple task of locating your car battery. But do not worry. I will still take good care of you for the rest of your life!* So I looked a third time. Strike three.

I remembered that some cars were designed with the battery located in the trunk. After making my way to the trunk, I began pulling stuff out. I eventually found the spare tire and the jack. Everything that was not physically attached to the car was removed from the trunk. The battery was nowhere to be found! At this point, I was ticked. *What idiot would design a car like this? Who has time to play hide and seek with a car battery? Ugh!!!*

My next move was to prove my competence to Melissa. After going inside, I began to vent my frustration. "Babe, some idiot designed your car with a hidden battery! I've looked under the hood and inside the trunk and the battery is nowhere to be found", I exclaimed. Now you need to understand something about Melissa. She is a genius. She calmly replied, "Seth, have you looked in the owner's manual to find the battery?" *What a great idea!*

After reading the owner's manual, locating the battery was a breeze. Changing the battery was a different story. In case you ever have to change a 1996 Dodge Stratus car battery, it is located above the driver's side tire. I recommend stretching and working on your flexibility before attempting that task. And I'm still not a fan of whoever designed the car that way.

There are two kinds of people in this world: people who read the instructions and people who do not. I have already revealed which type of person I tend to be. If I face a situation that requires reading an owner's manual, I use it as a last resort. For some reason, I enjoy trying to figure things out as I go. Life seems more fun that way. Melissa is the opposite. She will read the owner's manual first. For this reason, she does much better with tasks requiring assembly.

Which type of person are you? Do you read the instructions first? Or do you push them aside, leaving them as a last resort? You know, it is one thing to push an owner's manual aside. You may face some difficulty and frustration from time to time. But it is a totally different scenario when a person refuses to follow God's design for their marriage. You see, the Bible is God's Word. It is our instructions for living the life that God designed us to live. God created us and He understands how we are wired. So it is crucial for us to follow His instructions.

What would your marriage look like if you followed God's instructions? What would your marriage be like if you lived as though you believed God's Word? What kind of spouse could you be? What kind of parent could you be? What kind of life would your children enjoy? God's Word answers these questions in Psalm chapter 1:

"Blessed is the man who does not walk in the counsel of the wicked or stand in the way of sinners or sit in the seat of mockers. But his delight is in the law of the LORD and on his law he meditates day and night. He is like a tree planted by streams of water, which yields its fruit in season and whose leaf does not wither. Whatever he does prospers." - Psalm 1:1-3

This passage kicks off with the phrase, 'Blessed is the man'. Do you want to be blessed in life? I do! If you were to poll a large group of people, most of them would confess that they want to be blessed. Although most people say they want to be blessed, they do not feel blessed. Instead of experiencing God's best, they are settling for something less. In fact, many of these people do not even realize that there is more to life than their daily routine.

As these people clock in and out of each mundane task, God offers so much more. He wants our lives to unfold at the fullest measure possible. Why would we settle for something less than God's best? What would cause us to refuse His blessings? We have taken our eyes off God's instructions. Sadly, most husbands and wives have fallen into one of Satan's deadly traps. Psalm 1 highlights 3 common traps that we have a tendency of falling into. In fact, you may find yourself living in one today. The traps are progressive, each one leading to the next. It is crucial to recognize each one and get out as quickly as possible. Each trap is like glue. The longer you stay, the harder it is to break free. Let's take a look at verse one:

"Blessed is the man who does not walk in the counsel of the wicked or stand in the way of sinners or sit in the seat of mockers." - Psalm 1:1

Trap #1 Walking in the Counsel of the Wicked

What is the counsel of the wicked? It is any advice that comes from the world. The counsel of the wicked goes against the instructions of God's Word. This is a very deceptive trap, for much of the counsel of the wicked can make sense to us. Proverbs 14:12 says, *"There is a way that seems right to man, but in the end it leads to death."* The counsel of the wicked comes in many forms: television, movies, music, internet and people. Satan will use any means possible to steer us from God's path for our marriage and family. Our enemy does not want us to receive God's best. Who do you go to for advice? When you need direction, who do you lend an ear to? If that person is not walking in the instruction of God's Word, do not listen to their opinions. No matter how reasonable the advice may appear, do not take it to heart. The counsel of the wicked will take your marriage down paths that you were never meant to go.

Trap #2 Standing in the Way of the Sinner

When we listen to the counsel of the wicked, we begin taking on their ways. Advice is conformed into words and actions. We become active participants in behaviors that are sinful. These sinful behaviors can lead to strong habits, even addictions. Sin hurts people and separates us from intimacy with God. It will hurt our hearts and the hearts of others. Sin will literally rip our families apart. As sinful habits form, they become strongholds that are difficult to escape. Old habits are hard to break. We fall into this trap when we conform to the behaviors of people living in opposition to God's ways. We talk like them and walk like them. Our lives become an imitation of the wicked. We become like them, often without realizing what is taking place.

Trap #3 Sitting in the Seat of Mockers

This trap is rock bottom. Those who live in this trap have become grizzled in life. They are extremely negative toward others. Their hearts are calloused by the painful consequences of their sin. By listening to the counsel of the wicked and applying sinful practices, they have become experts at failure. They can tell you 101 reasons that you will fail but cannot show you one successful path to take. As they live in the realm of rock bottom, they make great effort to pull others down. Selfishness is their primary motivation in life. They are miserable and want others to feel miserable, too.

God is sovereign and He sits on His heavenly throne. He is all-powerful, all-knowing and is Lord over all. His very tongue spoke the cosmos into being! Those who sit in the seat of mockers do not recognize God's sovereignty. In fact, the seat of mockers has become their throne. In essence, they have become their own god. Their prideful eyes blind them to God's presence and the possibility of having a relationship with Him. And their sinful practices block their ears to God's instructions. Mockers are the know-it-alls of society. They laugh at anyone who acknowledges God, bowing down to their own selfish desires. In their minds, they are always right. When things don't go their way, they will quickly blame other people or circumstances for their failure. They make great effort to remove all responsibility from their lives.

Psalm 1:1 tells us that we will be blessed if we avoid these 3 traps. This verse clearly tells us what we should *not* do. When we avoid these traps, we will be free to experience great joy, purpose and friendship with God. Our marriages will experience more satisfaction. And our minds will be open to follow God's instructions in verses 2 and 3.

Taking Delight In God's Word

"But his delight is in the law of the LORD and on his law he meditates day and night. He is like a tree planted by streams of water, which yields its fruit in season and whose leaf does not wither. " - Psalm 1:2-3

These verses describe the life of a person who takes delight in God's Word. Instead of following the counsel of the wicked, applying their evil ways or mocking others, this person seeks God's counsel. Their minds are filled with good thoughts as they meditate on God's desires. Romans 12:2 says, *"Do not conform any longer to the patterns of this world but be transformed by the renewing of your mind."* Blessed people listen to God's instructions and apply His counsel to their lives. Their minds become renewed as they grow in God's ways. God's blessing overflows into all areas of life: marriage, parenting, family, friendships, finances, career, ministry and hobbies.

This passage provides a wonderful word picture. A person who receives God's blessing is like a tree that never dies. The leaves are always green, and the roots are always strong. It is always living for its created purpose. It grows, provides shade and bears fruit when it is time to do so. And it's fruit is sweet to the taste. This tree benefits all life around it.

One of my favorite past-times is to take prayer walks with God. It is so refreshing to get away from the noise of life. One of my favorite places to walk is called the Greenway. This is a beautiful set of paths that follow a river and winds through Florida swamp ponds. You can see all kinds of birds, fish, fiddler crabs, turtles and alligators. I feel so relaxed there.

I especially enjoy walking along the Greenway on cloudy days. There are some trees that grow along the riverbanks. When the gray clouds cover the brightness of the sun, the water looks dim. The clouds provide a gray background for everything. Although the sky and water seem lifeless, the trees seem to explode with color. The green leaves jump out from the gray and dim background, seeming to shout 'I'm alive!'

Life can be difficult at times. Sometimes things do not go the way we had hoped. The storms of life can make our day to day survival gray and dim. Although the storms bring difficulty, they also bring opportunity. Blessed people are the ones who shine during the storms. Their attitude brings refreshment. And their words and actions shout "I am alive!" Blessed people carry a contagious joy. We just want to be around them.

The Promise

My favorite part of Psalm 1:1-3 is the ending. God gives us a promise. And when God promises something, you can take it to the bank. He is true to His Word! Psalm 1:3 closes by describing the life of a blessed person. God says, *"Whatever he does will prosper."* What a promise! When you follow God's instructions, whatever you do will prosper. You cannot lose! For God will even take your failure and work it for His good purposes. God wants to bless *all* parts of your life, not some areas or most areas. Understand that God is making a bold claim here. And He is waiting to see if you will take His offer.

So here is the promise: If we avoid Satan's traps and follow God's instructions, then our lives will prosper. It is really that simple. How do we receive God's promise? The primary difference between God's best and a second rate life rests in a choice. If we follow God's instructions, everything we do will prosper. But if we ignore God's instructions, we will become experts at failure.

Your choice is simple. Will you obey God's instructions? It seems like an easy decision to me. But the decision is yours to make. Understand that your choice will not only affect your life. It will determine the present and future of your marriage, too. So choose wisely.

Under Attack

"Our struggle is not against flesh and blood, but against the rulers, against the authorities, against the powers of this dark world and against the spiritual forces of evil in the heavenly realms. Therefore put on the full armor of God, so that when the day of evil comes, you may be able to stand your ground." - Ephesians 6:12-13

On September 11th, 2001 the United States experienced a deadly terrorist attack. Our nation was stunned as we watched the nightmare unfold. On that Tuesday morning, terrorists from the Al-Qaeda militant group hijacked four passenger jets. American Airlines Flight 11 and United Airlines Flight 175 were intentionally driven into the Twin Towers of the World Trade Center in New York City. Within a couple of hours, both of the towers crumbled to the ground.

Terrorists also crashed American Airlines Flight 77 into the Pentagon in Arlington, VA. As the deadly attack continued to unfold, United Airlines Flight 93 crashed in a field in Shanksville, Pennsylvania. The passengers managed to take control of the fourth jet before it reached its destination in Washington, D.C. As our nation watched in horror, almost 3,000 people lost their lives.

The United States responded to our enemies by proclaiming the War on Terror. As the war progressed, the responsible terrorist leader emerged through our media. Osama bin Laden's face was well known by 2004, as he proclaimed a victory in the September 11th attacks.

The search for this terrorist leader was in full force for many years. Our military never gave up the search for the man who led a successful invasion on our homeland. Osama bin Laden was located and killed in May of 2011. For the first time in ten years, the United States could breathe a sigh of relief. One of our nation's enemies was taken down.

I can still remember what September 11th 2001 was like. At the time, I was a student pastor. That day began like a normal day. I woke up, ate some breakfast and prepared for the ministry tasks to be accomplished.

On my way to the church office, my Dad recognized my car. He quickly signaled for me to pull over. "A jet has crashed into one of the Twin Towers!", he exclaimed. Understand that I was still in the process of waking up. So the reality of that statement soared over my head. As my Dad drove away, I continued my drive to the church office. My plan was to catch an early lunch and watch the news for details of the jet crash. Even the thought of a possible terrorist attack never crossed my mind.

The church phone began ringing off the hook. And our answering machine was full of messages. The next few hours were filled with phone conversations with church members and seemingly random people in our community. Each person was calling out of fear and wanted to pray for our country's safety. Through those conversations, my eyes were opened to reality. Our nation was under a terrorist attack.

The scariest part of September 11th was the fact that it caught us off guard. We simply didn't see it coming. As we were rubbing the sleep out of our eyes, the terrorists were making their move. By the time our nation realized what was happening, the damage was already done. Our nation was totally blind-sided by the terrible events of that day.

Although the Taliban terrorists struck fear into our hearts, there is a greater enemy that we face. This enemy not only endangers families in the United States, but all across the world. He despises all people and he loves to blind-side us. His hatred extends to all nations. He has been terrorizing families in every generation, from the beginning of time. Our homes are not immune to his attack. At any given moment, he can strike. God's Word speaks of the danger we face...

"Do not give the devil a foothold." - *Ephesians 4:27*

"Your enemy the devil prowls around like a roaring lion looking for someone to devour." - *1 Peter 5:8*

"Our struggle is not against flesh and blood, but against the rulers, against the authorities, against the powers of this dark world and against the spiritual forces of evil in the heavenly realms. Therefore put on the full armor of God, so that when the day of evil comes, you may be able to stand your ground." - *Ephesians 6:12-13*

Satan hates you. He hates me. Satan hates all people. He is the greatest enemy that you will ever face. He is not some fantasy character, dressed in red and carrying a pitch fork. He is real. And his goal is to rip your family apart, one by one. Both your marriage and children are on his radar. Your home is not safe. You can lock your doors and install the best security system on the market, but it will not keep him out. Satan comes fully loaded with a monstrous legion of demons. Countless families fall prey to his army daily. He is watching and lurking. His army never rests. No family is immune to this present danger. We are in a war.

You must guard your marriage and children from Satan's attack. How can you stand against him? One of the first steps toward guarding your family is to understand Satan's strategy. By understanding his strategy, you can be better prepared for his attacks. You can be equipped to stand firm and protect those you love most. So what is Satan's strategy? The book of John clearly answers this question. John 10:10 says, *"The thief comes to steal, kill and destroy."* This verse calls Satan a thief and rightly so.

Perhaps your family has already experienced pain from Satan's attacks. Maybe your marriage is lacking or you feel like a failure in parenting. Perhaps your heart has been broken by the tearing of a divorce. As you hold this book, I want to encourage you. No matter what you've said or what you've done or how many times you have failed to protect your family from Satan's attack, there is hope. Turn to God. God is the God of restoration. He will meet you where you are. Although you will always live with consequences of your actions, God will begin to heal your heart. He wants you and your family to walk with Him. Zephaniah 3:17 says, *"The LORD your God is with you. He is mighty to save. He will take great delight in you, he will quiet you with His love, He will rejoice over you with singing."* Let those words sink in. You are loved by God and so is your family. No matter what your family looks like today, God wants to use you to stand guard for them.

As I mentioned earlier, Satan's strategy is to steal, kill and destroy the life of your family. He has put great thought into his strategy so his execution is highly effective. Satan's primary target is your marriage. He knows that if he can tear apart your marriage, your children will be easy prey. As you read through the rest of this chapter, take some time to pause and reflect. Recognize where Satan has attacked in the past and where he may be moving now. Understand that he moves in subtle ways. It requires great intention to recognize a possible attack. The key is to go on the defense as early as possible. Once he gains a foothold, it is more difficult to remove his influence. Here are three specific ways that Satan will attempt to un-leash his venom into your marriage and family.

1. Satan wants to *steal* your joy

Matt and Jenny are newly weds. They invested countless hours and resources in their wedding ceremony and reception. The reception was followed by an amazing honeymoon. Butterflies seemed to fill their hearts as they enjoyed these first steps into their new life together. These beginning weeks were packed with exciting talks about the future. In their minds, the sky was the limit.

As they return from the honeymoon, they begin to settle into their new life. Weekly routines return as Matt and Jenny step back into the reality of a busy schedule. Matt works an average of 45 hours per week. Jenny also works full-time. Matt volunteers to coach children through their community basketball league. Jenny enjoys singing for the praise team at church. She also serves as a Sunday school teacher. This leaves limited opportunity for time together. After four months of busy schedules, Matt and Jenny take note of the lack of time they enjoy with one another.

As they sit down to plan some date nights, they notice the bills. Rent, water, electric, credit cards, trash pick-up, phone, internet, health insurance, life insurance, student loans and the first monthly bill for ring payments roll in. These bills do not even include money for gas and food! Matt's blood pressure suddenly rises. Jenny's stress level shoots up. Suddenly, Matt remembers some needed car repairs. Where would the money for date nights come from? And how in the world will they pay each of these bills?

Matt and Jenny are entering the danger zone. They feel like victims to their busy schedules and financial stress. The chains weigh heavy upon their shoulders. If they are like most couples, they will allow their joy to slip from their hearts. The stress will lead to outbursts and heated arguments as they allow the enemy to steal their joy.

2. Satan wants to *kill* marital intimacy

At this point, Matt and Jenny notice that something seems to be wrong in their marriage. The butterflies have taken flight from their hearts. When they look at each other, they no longer feel that intimate connection they shared before. Their intimate connection has been replaced with frustration.

As the number of arguments increase, the kind words decrease. Their communication becomes harsh as they often speak exactly what is on their mind. Matt and Jenny find multiple topics of disagreement. Matt wants to paint the interior of their home blue. Jenny wants to have multiple colors throughout the house. Matt thinks Jenny should wash the dishes while Jenny expects Matt to help. Jenny hopes to have three children while Matt only wants one. Matt plans to discipline their future child through spankings but Jenny wants to use time out techniques. And the list goes on.

Instead of resolving their disagreements, they simply agree to disagree. Both assume that the other one's perspective will change in the future. Each topic of disagreement becomes a wall in their relationship. The topic is closed for discussion. Matt and Jenny can talk about anything in life except the topics of disagreement.

This seems to fix things at first. As newly weds, they are still getting to know one another. So they still have countless topics they can discuss. But as more disagreements arise, more walls are built. As time rolls on, Matt and Jenny find that their conversation is extremely limited. Communication becomes awkward as they struggle to find common topics to discuss. For the first time in their marriage, they begin having doubts. They wonder if their marriage was a mistake. So they begin contemplating thoughts of divorce. The enemy is in the process of killing their intimacy.

3. Satan wants to *destroy* your future

Matt and Jenny's thoughts of divorce become vocal as they experience more heated arguments. As tempers rise, Jenny shouts, "I don't know why I married you!" Matt responds by screaming, "I don't know who you are anymore!" Then one of them crosses the line. "We should just get a divorce." Those words seem even more painful than the thoughts. Both of them feel betrayed, hurt and angry. Their unconditional love has now become conditional.

Both Matt and Jenny vent their frustrations with friends and family. Jenny becomes the enemy of Matt's family and Matt becomes the enemy of Jenny's family. Matt becomes a walking testimony of Proverbs 18:13. He shows what happens when a man *"answers before listening- that is his folly and shame."* His unloving words drive a wedge in his marriage. Jenny becomes a real life illustration of Proverbs 14:1 *"The wise woman builds her house; but with her own hands the foolish one tears hers down."* Jenny's disrespectful behavior causes Matt to stone wall her. Although he may be in the same room physically, his heart is cold toward her.

As the stress and pain increase, Matt decides to take action. His eyes wonder to other women as he seeks attention from them. He reasons that every man has sexual needs. Since Jenny was no longer meeting his sexual needs, then it would be acceptable to allow another woman to do so. One thing leads to another as Matt finds himself lost in the lust of another woman. He feels important with her. The other woman helps Matt feel respected. This causes him to want her even more.

Jenny suspects that Matt may be cheating on her. When she confronts him, Matt denies it. With more pushing, Matt finally confesses. What was left of Jenny's heart was shattered to pieces. As Matt proclaims his right to feel respected by a woman, Jenny begins to weep. She knows that the marriage is over. The next morning, their future is destroyed through divorce papers. The divorce seems to be an easy solution to their marriage problems. In reality, they have no idea what they will experience. This is only the beginning of a long road of relational wounds and scars they will carry with them. Satan's demons applaud as one more couple's future is destroyed.

Jenny and Matt represent countless couples today. Although the names and faces change, the stories seem to follow the same pattern. A couple enters marriage with big dreams and a wonderful hope. Without realizing Satan's attacks, they get lost in busy schedules and growing financial stress. As Satan steals their joy, major disagreements arise. Instead of working through their differences, the couple agrees to disagree. In doing so, they construct relational walls and their communication becomes restricted. As conversation becomes limited, the couple will lose intimacy and grow apart. Satan enjoys destroying marriages.

It is time for husbands and wives to wake up and recognize Satan's attack! We must identify where he is attacking and kick him out immediately. We are responsible for guarding our marriages. Stand up, Husbands! Arise, Wives! Hold tightly to your joy. Defend your marriage intimacy at all cost. And look to the future with a great hope. We can do this!

"For nothing is impossible with God." - Luke 1:37

Aftermath: Our Wounded Generation

"The LORD is slow to anger, abounding in love and forgiving sin and rebellion. Yet he does not leave the guilty unpunished; he punishes the children for the sin of the fathers to the third and fourth generation."
- Numbers 14:18

I've always had an intense competitive streak. The intensity was greater during my childhood and adolescent years. Although it has diminished since then, I still enjoy some friendly competition. Whether I'm playing a game of cards or a pick-up game of basketball, I'm known for a little trash talk here and there.

During my senior year of college I played on a city league basketball team. It was made up of some guys I grew up with. On one particular Friday evening, I had an early game. Following the game, I had a lock-in to attend at the church I served as student pastor. With strategic planning, my youth ministry team would handle the opening activities and I would arrive to preach later in the evening.

Before the basketball game tipped off, I made my coach a promise. "Whether we win or lose this game, you can expect total hustle from me," I assured my coach. "When you think back on this game, you will always remember that Seth Widner hustled!" I jokingly added.

As the game began, I gave it my all. Within the first two minutes of the game, I became glue to the man I guarded. Although he tried, I would not allow him to get open. Suddenly one of my teammates slapped an attempted pass in mid air, sending the ball rolling down the court. I ran as hard as I could toward the ball. As I bent down to scoop it up, one of the other team's players accidentally tripped me from behind. I stumbled at full speed into a block wall. The crazy thing is that I didn't feel any pain at the time!

The pain came later. As I enjoyed my ambulance ride to the hospital, my head began to ache. This didn't surprise me since it was bleeding upon impact. I was surprised by the growing pain in my wrists. After being examined at the hospital, I learned that I suffered a concussion, cracked both wrists and my scalp received seven staples to close an open wound. By the time I reached the lock-in, the pain level was great and I was fully aware of the impact the wall had on my body.

Just like my basketball injury, divorce brings pain. Although some of the pain is immediate, sometimes the full extent of pain is not recognized until a later time. During the process of divorce, husbands and wives feel anger toward one another. Anger has a way of distracting them from pain.

Confusion fills the hearts of the children. In an effort to protect, moms and dads try to guard their children's ears from the reality of divorce. They may pretend like everything is ok, stating that the new living conditions will be better for their family. Children are like sponges. Although they may not fully understand the facts, they will absorb the emotions of their parents. When they take on the emotions without understanding, fear may take root in their little hearts.

As the smoke clears from the divorce process, adults and children must face a new reality. Their eyes now face an aftermath of broken pieces they once considered as family. For decades, countless families have suffered through the vicious cycle of divorce. One of the outcomes we now face is a wounded generation. Both adults and children carry deep relational wounds that can cripple all areas of life.

Robert Lewis has recognized our wounded generation. He created a strategic ministry to help men deal with the pain of their past and chase after God's great purpose for them. His ministry is called Men's Fraternity. Men's Fraternity is a three year course that helps men identify their manhood wounds and address them. I recommend his curriculum to every church to purchase! I also recommend Robert Lewis' 33 Series. This is a revised DVD series that highlights the manhood wounds and principles from Men's Fraternity. (www.mensfraternity.com) (33theseries.com)

In "Men's Fraternity," Robert highlights five common wounds that need to be addressed. I've selected two of the wounds to highlight in this chapter. Although Robert focuses on how these wounds affect the lives of boys and men, he also recognizes that girls and women now suffer from them, too. As I walk through the common wounds below, understand that I am writing to both genders. As you read through them, be sure to take note of the one(s) that you identify in your life. The first step toward healing is to acknowledge the wound.

The Absent Father Wound

Many people have grown up without their father in the home. And for those whose father lived in the home, he was often emotionally absent. This cycle has been going on for generations. For this reason, our nation is currently facing a manhood crises. We have three generations of men who have no idea what it means to be a good husband or father. Today's generation of husbands and wives lack the example of a solid male role model to influence them for the good. Therefore this deadly wound is being passed on to our children.

This wound seems to affect boys and girls differently. Boys are left with an incomplete definition of masculinity. They end up coming up with their own definition of a husband and father. Sadly, these self made definitions are far from God's design. Boys who are forced to create an incomplete definition of masculinity will lack a foundation to build a healthy marriage and family.

Girls have a deep longing to feel cherished. When their father fails to cherish them, girls will seek to have this need met by other boys and men. These girls often lack discernment of character. Their intense desire to feel cherished can blind their eyes to flawed character. They may compromise their body and reputation for the opportunity to be held in someone's arms. Let me give you some common ways I've witnessed this wound play out in peoples' lives.

A Girl's Story:

Tiffany's parents were divorced when she was eight. From that time on, she rarely heard from her father. Although she had the support of her mother, she longed for the embrace of her father. Occasionally she would receive word that he would attend a birthday party or special event at school. This expectation would get her hopes up. But his face was never seen. Tiffany would feel rejected and carried a lot of resentment.

Tiffany's teenage years were characterized by countless boyfriends. She became sexually active at thirteen. In time, she developed the pattern of running to any boy who showed interest in her. She would overlook serious character flaws in each of these young men. As long as they gave her attention, she would give them anything they wanted.

She became pregnant at nineteen and chose to marry her boyfriend. Although he wasn't necessarily her knight in shining armor, she wanted her child to have a father. Over time he became verbally abusive toward her. Despite his dangerous behavior, Tiffany stayed with him. Each day she would wake up, hoping that her marriage would become healthy. But it never did.

After giving birth to her second child, her husband left her for another woman. He told Tiffany that he was no longer attracted to her. Once again, Tiffany is abandoned by a man. The pain reminds her of the wound she received long ago, when her father walked out on her mother and her. As she looks into the eyes of her children, she is broken. She realizes that her children will also grow up without a father.

A Boy's Story:

Kenny's mother became pregnant with him at the age of seventeen. His father bolted when he found out about the pregnancy. His mother lacked the means of taking care of him. So his grandparents stepped in as the primary caregivers. Although his physical needs were met, his emotional needs were not. His mother cared more about her social status and school parties than spending time with Kenny. His grandparents were simply tired. Kenny wasn't exactly the retirement plan they had hoped for.

As Kenny grew up, he longed for the presence of his father. He often wondered how he could miss someone he never met. His heart ached each time he saw his friends go fishing or camping with their father. He felt rejected, like something was wrong with him.

Kenny decided to lock the pain away and move on. He wanted to create the family he never had. During his teenage years, he rushed into relationships quickly. He was like a football player running onto the field, forgetting to put on his pads or helmet. After the first collision of conflict, he found himself in a great deal of pain. He would quickly give away his heart only to have it broken.

After years of failed relationship attempts, Kenny gives up his desire to have a family. He simply conforms to the culture's false images of masculinity. He turns to alcohol to numb his pain, as he spends his evenings in the arms of one-night stands. His goal is to forget the past and live in the present. His mind gives little thought to the choices he makes today.

Over the years, Kenny becomes the father of several children. He knows about some of his children but is unsure how many he actually has fathered. He spends his days hiding from his growing debt of unpaid child support while looking for a woman who can heal the pain in his heart. His life expresses the definition of insanity. He walks down the same road of destruction, expecting different results.

The Overly Bonded With Mother Wound

This wound is inflicted by well-meaning mothers. Since so many fathers are absent in the homes, the mother is left to provide for the needs of her children. She is forced to play the role of both father and mother. No matter how hard she tries, she was never designed to carry this burden. Asking a mother to be a father is a cruel request. It sets her up for failure. It is a task that she cannot accomplish, no matter how hard she tries.

Children who grow up under the influence of this wound are overly nurtured. Although these mothers have great intentions, they struggle to release their control over their children. As the children grow up, they will either resent their mother's control or simply accept it.

How does this wound affect men and women? Adults carrying this wound tend to live out one of two extremes in their relationships. They will either be overly controlling or overly passive. If they are controlling, they will not allow their mother to be a part of their life. Their hearts will be filled with resentment toward her. And they make great effort to control all other relationships they hold.

Adults can also respond to this wound by being overly passive. They will carry their mother's influence with them wherever they go. They lack initiative in setting healthy boundaries. Their passive behavior will drive their future spouse crazy. The mother will make great effort to control her child's marriage, career and finances. She will strive to maintain a voice in all areas of life. And the adult who used to be her child will allow her to have her way. The wound is like a stamp on the forehead that says 'Door Mat'.

Time To Unpack Things

The Absent Father and Overly Bonded with Mother wound have been damaging marriages for decades. Husbands and wives are often clueless to the wounds in their hearts. Do you suffer from one of these wounds? How is this wound affecting your marriage and family today?

I recently enjoyed a vacation in Tennessee. It was refreshing to get away and spend time with family and friends. Although I love taking vacations, I cannot stand the sight of my suitcase! Packing and unpacking are two tasks I tend to avoid. You see, I'm a last minute packer. I cannot stand this task! And the only thing worse than packing is un-packing. At least the task of packing comes with thoughts of an upcoming vacation. As I return from a vacation, I will procrastinate when it comes to unpacking. Instead of removing all my clothes from the suitcase at one time, I will simply pull out things to wear daily. This process can literally continue for weeks!

Many people seem to relate with me on this topic. It seems that people don't enjoy unpacking. This is true with suitcases and emotional baggage. As people, we all carry relational wounds and scars from the past. These wounds need to be addressed. If left unattended, each wound will affect our marriages and families. We will simply pass on our pain to our spouse and children. Our ability to unpack our past will determine the level of success or failure we will experience as husbands, wives, mothers and fathers. So it's time to unpack things. If you are ready to overcome your emotional scars and wounds, follow these steps:

1. **Identify Your Pain.** Psalm 147:3 says, *"He heals the brokenhearted and binds up their wounds."* The first step toward healing is to acknowledge your pain. Since this can be a scary thing to do, let me share some encouraging truth with you. God is the One who can heal you. He not only holds the power to heal, God *wants* to heal your heart! He loves you and wants to heal your wounds.

2. **Give Your Pain To Christ**. Psalm 55:22 says, *"Cast your cares on the LORD and He will sustain you."* 1 Peter 5:7 says, *"Cast all your anxiety on Him because He cares for you."* Do you want to overcome your pain? Open your heart to the One who can heal you. Tell Christ how you feel and acknowledge how your pain is affecting you. He will listen. As you talk to Him, give it all to Him. Your shoulders were not meant to carry that heavy load by yourself. Release your pain to Christ. His shoulders are big enough to carry your burdens.

3. **Forgive**. Many people do not understand the concept of   biblical forgiveness. So let me clarify

what is involved with biblical forgiveness. When you forgive someone, you are not saying *"We are ok now."* You are literally saying, *"I am not going to hold any feelings of anger or resentment toward you. I choose to allow God to be the judge between you and me."* Sometimes forgiveness can lead to reconciling a broken relationship and sometimes it doesn't. But forgiveness always releases you from the chains of resentment. And it opens the door to ongoing fellowship with Christ. Matthew 6:14-15 says, *"If you forgive men when they sin against you, your heavenly Father will also forgive you. But if you do not forgive men their sins, your Father will not forgive your sins."* Our God is a righteous judge.

If you suffer from the Absent Father Wound, forgive your father. If you suffer from the Overly Bonded With Mother Wound, cut the cord. Set some boundaries that establish yourself as an adult. And forgive your mother. Release that anger and let the resentment go.

4. **Break the Generational Chains.** Perhaps your wounds come from generational sins. It is common for the Absent Father and Overly Bonded With Mother wounds to be passed down to the next generation. In Exodus 20:5-6, God says that He is *"punishing the children for the sins of the fathers to the third and*

45

fourth generation of those who hate me, but showing love to a thousand generations of those who love me and keep my commandments." Maybe your wound was initiated by a distant relative's disobedience to God and the pain has been passed down to you. Perhaps your family tree feels cursed. You are experiencing the first part of the above verses. But you do not have to pass that pain to your spouse and children. You can choose to change! By following God's commands, you will be positioning yourself for a new season of life. He promises to show His *"love to a thousand generations of those who love"* Him. So go ahead. Break those chains. Freedom is one step away.

5. Be different. Instead of following the sinful ways of previous generations, choose to live differently. Start a new legacy for your family tree! No matter what you have said or what you have done, you are only one decision away from the good! Deuteronomy paints a beautiful picture of a blessed family tree. It portrays what a family can look like when we follow God's design.

As this chapter draws to a close, spend a few minutes reading through the following verses. Allow Christ to show you some practical ways to live them out. Do not be like the previous generations. Instead of passing your wound on to your spouse and children, give them Christ's love instead. If you follow God's lead, you will leave a lasting legacy for the generations to come! So choose to be different. Walk in Christ's love, and pass it on.

"Love the LORD your God with all your heart and with all your soul and with all your strength. These commandments that I give you today are to be upon your hearts. Impress them upon your children. Talk about them when you sit at home and when you walk along the road, when you lie down and when you get up. Tie them as symbols on your hands and bind them on your foreheads. Write them on the doorframes of your houses and on your gates." - Deuteronomy 6:5-9

Returning to God's Design

"Return to the LORD...that He may return to you. Do not be like your fathers and brothers who were unfaithful to the LORD, the God of their fathers. Do not be stiff-necked, as your fathers were. Submit to the LORD."
- 2 Chronicles 30:6-8

When couples ask me to officiate their wedding, I get excited for them. Their hearts feel the butterflies of romance and they hold great hopes for the future. Their words and body language proclaim "We are in love!" They want to spend the rest of their lives together. Being engaged is a wonderful season of life.

Sometimes it throws couples off when I share my pre-requisite for officiating weddings. Some pastors require a high financial fee. They do this for good reason. The financial sacrifice determines if the couple wants to get married. For most people will make great sacrifice for something they really want. The fee also helps compensate the pastor's time and resources.

My pre-requisite doesn't involve a financial sacrifice. Rather, I require a sacrifice of time. Before I agree to officiate a wedding, the couple must walk through 6-8 weeks of premarital counsel with me. In each hourly session, we focus on God's design for marriage.

Some couples are taken back by this. One couple actually pointed out the fact that I was requiring more than the law. For the law allows, in most states, that a couple can get a discount on the marriage license by completing three hours of approved premarital counsel. My response is simple. I explain that love requires sacrifice. And my goal is to prepare couples to experience God's best rather than gain a discount on the marriage license.

As a family pastor, I also see what happens when couples do not follow God's design. When couples reach out for help, I hear their stories. Wives weep and husbands hurt. They drop their pain in my office as they explain their difficulties. Their hearts are broken and lost in a sea of pain. Wives point out the unloving behavior of their husbands. And husbands proclaim the disrespectful words of their wives. These couples are crying out for something more. They are desperately reaching for hope, wondering if it even exists.

Although I love helping couples, I'm tired. I'm tired of hearing the horror stories of pain and regret. I'm tired of seeing the fingers pointing the blame on the other spouse. "It is your fault!" they declare. I'm tired of witnessing two adults regress into children as the temper-tantrums unfold. I'm tired of children's hearts being eaten by the destruction of divorce, as their parents expect them to choose sides. And I'm tired of seeing little difference between Christian couples and nonChristian couples. It makes me sick. My head is pounding from their cries, and my heart breaks for them.

So what keeps me going? What would motivate me to continue reaching out to couples? I would answer these questions with one word. Hope. That is a refreshing reality to cling to! As couples share their pain, I am clinging to hope. It excites me. It propels me. Hope keeps me going. For I know that every couple has hope. And that hope is well within their reach.

A Story Of Hope

James and Rachel grew up in church. They heard the Bible stories and made great friendships with fellow believers. James' parents were faithful in attendance. If the church doors were open, his family was likely to be there. He was active in his church from birth.

Rachel's family connected to their church when she was about ten. Once they connected, they became very active in church life. Her parents served on ministry teams and enjoyed taking mission trips together every other year. They even helped plan the annual V.B.S. programs.

On the surface level, one would think that their families were great models to be followed. In reality, there were some things happening behind the scenes. Rachel's parents had heated disagreements and her father would leave home for days at a time. Her mother would express her frustrations to the children while her father was away. When her father returned, they would act as if everything was ok. This pattern of conflict continued until Rachel left home for college. While she was in college, her parents finally threw in the towel.

James' parents struggled financially. His mother coped by hiding in a busy schedule and his father hit the bottle. By the time James was in high school, his parents separated for about two weeks. During that separation, his father had an affair. When James' mother found out about the affair, the marriage ended. Although his father justified the affair by stating that they were separated at the time, all trust was broken. Their marriage ended in divorce.

Both James and Rachel held a deep desire to be different from their parents. They wanted to have a marriage built to last. Sadly, both experienced several failed marriages before meeting one another.

When I met James and Rachel, they were engaged to be married. Both were glowing with excitement. James had been married four times and Rachel had been married twice. They wanted their upcoming marriage to be different. James proclaimed, "I want to get this one right!" Rachel responded by sharing her desire for a healthy marriage. Both of them confessed that their previous marriages lacked the foundation of Christ. As I heard their stories, I agreed.

After forty-five minutes of sharing, James and Rachel paused. They looked at me and asked a common question. "Is there hope for us to have a great marriage?" Rachel asked. I began to grin from ear to ear and leaned forward with my response. "Yes!"

Hope exists for every couple who will follow God's design for marriage. One of the things I have learned is that most people, even Christians, do not fully understand God's design for marriage. People pick up bits and pieces over the years and make effort to apply what they know. But these bits and pieces are not enough! In order for you to experience a healthy marriage, you must commit to following God's design. Not some of it. You must follow all of it. When you do, God will prove Himself faithful.

God's Design For Marriage

What is God's design for marriage? Husbands and wives must live as one flesh. The two must become one. Everything we say and do must be in alignment with one another. This design has been around since the beginning of time. In Genesis chapter two, God created the first marriage: Adam and Eve. As Eve was given to Adam, God proclaimed that everything was very good. God also established His design for their marriage. In Genesis 2:24, God says *"For this reason, a man will leave his father and mother and be united to his wife, and they will become one flesh."*

In our culture, living as one is a foreign concept. We are taught to be strong and independent. We should never place ourselves in a position to depend on another person. In fact, most people view the concept of being dependent upon someone as a major weakness. So we enter marriage as individuals. Be your own man! Be your own woman! Everything becomes *'His'* or *'Hers'* rather than *'Ours.'* This mentality is cancer to marriages.

We cannot go against God's design and expect His blessings. He is our Creator and understands what is best for us. Instead of running from His design, we must embrace it. By embracing God's design, we align ourselves to receive His blessings. One of His blessings will be a healthy marriage.

How can you practically live out God's design for your marriage? What would your marriage look like if you lived out His design? The answer can be found in Genesis 2:24. This powerful verse provides three needed steps toward living as one flesh.

1. **Leave** God proclaims that we must *leave* our father and mother. When we get married, our spouse becomes more important than any other person. Our allegiance is to our marriage. Your parents cease to provide for your needs. God has ordained your spouse as the one to meet your needs. And He wants you to meet the needs of your spouse. This does not mean that you can no longer have a relationship with your and father or mother. It simply means that your spouse now comes before them.

For most couples, this step involves setting some boundaries. And setting boundaries is easier said than done. This new marriage relationship requires adjustments from everyone. These adjustments can be especially hard for parents. Parents have established family traditions that have been playing out for decades. They have been celebrating holidays in specific ways. Each tradition has become close to the heart. And many parents expect you to keep their traditions. This expectation is easily seen around the holidays.

Change of tradition often involves some form of conflict. Families are used to doing things a specific way and now you are initiating a change. Who will you celebrate Thanksgiving and Christmas with? Whose church will you attend on Easter? Which Mom will enjoy a lunch on Mother's Day? Unless boundaries are established, you will feel like the rope in a tug of war match.

The earlier you establish boundaries, the better. Sit down with your spouse and develop a plan for setting the boundaries. You are a new family and will function differently! Choose which traditions you want to keep and which you'd like to change. Remember, your marriage has created a new family. You may want to keep some family traditions passed down from your parents. You may choose to create some brand new traditions. And some of your traditions will be a blending from your previous family traditions. You must make your own decisions. You are a new family!

When Melissa and I were first married, we still lived close to my parents and hers. Thanksgiving and Christmas seem to be the big holidays for our extended families. So we were faced with the question, *Who will we celebrate the holidays with?* Since our parents live so close together, we could practically spend each holiday with both sides of the family. But the thought of gorging ourselves on two big meals and rushing from one house to the other didn't appeal to us. So we set a boundary.

Each year, we spend Thanksgiving with one side of the family and Christmas with the other. Then we flip flop who we spend each holiday with the following year. We communicated our plans to both sides of our extended family. By setting the boundary early, our holidays are enjoyable!

The process of leaving your father and mother is not only physical. You will also need to evaluate some behaviors. More than likely, you have taken on some unhealthy behavioral patterns from your parents and grandparents. If your father and mother struggle in communication, you will have that tendency. If they struggle to resolve conflict, you will likely share that struggle. The traits of our parents are normally passed on to us. So examine your relational patterns. Highlight the behaviors that may hinder oneness with your spouse.

After recognizing unwanted behavior patterns, you must choose to leave them. If you continue to carry them into your marriage, both you and your spouse will suffer the consequences. Unhealthy behaviors can destroy a marriage. So choose wisely. Make a plan to leave those behaviors today.

Patience is needed during the process of leaving your father and mother. This process is a huge transition for many people. So be patient with yourself. And extend patience to your spouse.

2. **Unite**. We must be on the same page as husbands and wives. This union is physical, emotional, mental and spiritual. All areas of life will be lived out within the marriage relationship. God is bringing two different people together for life. So we will grow close in thought and behavior.

In most relationships, we enjoy the phrase '*We must agree to disagree*.' It allows friends and family to disagree while keeping the friendship in place. But marriage is different. It is the only human relationship that cannot operate under this mentality.

If you agree to disagree with your spouse, it can create a relational wall. That specific topic becomes a '*Do Not Enter*' zone for future conversations. You can talk about anything else in life, except that specific topic. Relational walls are not usually noticed during the first few months of marriage. For couples are still getting to know one another and have a variety of other topics they can talk about. But as time passes and the pattern of 'agreeing to disagree' continues to played out, it will be difficult for a couple to walk in unity. And unity is God's design for husbands and wives.

When you find areas of disagreement between you and your spouse, turn to God's Word. Instead of relying on your own thoughts and feelings, see what God says about the topic. Here are some common areas that can bring disagreement:

- *Finances*

- *Parenting*

- *Sex*

- *Values*

- *Family Roles*

God's design is for you to walk in unity with your spouse. Seek God's Word and work out those differences. Commit to obeying God's desires. It will promote growth and help you live in unity with your spouse.

3. **Become One Flesh**. This is God's ultimate goal for marriage. By following the previous steps, we will land here. When we leave our parents and walk in unity together, we will become one flesh. This is the closeness that we long for. No substitute can compensate for it. It is the deepest level of intimacy. Couples will literally live as one person. All areas of life will be experienced together. The common areas of disagreement will be conquered. We will walk hand in hand in our faith, finances, parenting, values, family roles, and sexual enjoyment.

Taking this step is not easy. For our culture teaches a false illusion of intimacy. We are taught that intimacy should be an easy path for healthy couples. The chick flicks of our day proclaim that oneness requires little effort with the one you are meant to be with. These are all lies! In reality, reaching and sustaining intimacy in marriage is a difficult process. True intimacy requires living uncomfortably close with another imperfect person.

What is uncomfortable about being close? James 3:2 says, *"We all stumble in many ways."* True intimacy requires full acceptance of one another. We must be open about our insecurities and weaknesses. Marital oneness requires accepting the good, the bad and the ugly.

How does your marriage compare with God's design for oneness? Understand the intent of this question is not to judge or condemn you. I want you to experience God's best! In order to reach for God's best, you must have a clear perspective of where you are today. God wants you to live as one flesh with your spouse. Although living as one flesh is not an easy road, it can be achieved. If God designed the road, He will empower us to drive upon it.

No matter what your marriage looks like today, there is hope for you. God's design works! I have never met a couple who said, "I lived out God's design for marriage and it ended in divorce." You are one decision away from the change you thirst for. And that decision is to return to God's design. Go ahead. Run to Him. He will meet you with open arms.

"If my people, who are called by my Name, will humble themselves and pray and seek my face and turn from their wicked ways, then I will hear from heaven and will forgive their sin and will heal their land."
- 2 Chronicles 7:14

Eliminate False Expectations

"Do not conform any longer to the pattern of this world, but be transformed by the renewing of your mind. Then you will be able to test and approve what God's will is- His good, pleasing and perfect will." - Romans 12:2

I will never forget the day I saw my first car. It was a beautiful sight for my sore eyes! My Dad and I had been to several car dealerships, looking for the right car within our price range. After a long and dedicated search, my eyes rested on the perfect car. *I can't believe this! I am going to own this sweet, jet-black sports car!* As I gazed upon that black beauty, I began to envision my climb up the popularity ladder. My high school would know me by name! Every babe in town would line up to ride with me.

As I turned that car on, she purred like a kitten. So we took her on a test drive. Since my Dad was in the car, I held off the gas pedal. He needed to believe that I was responsible. Although my foot treaded lightly on the pedal, I could tell there was a lot of power under the hood. By the time we got back to the dealership, my mind was made up. I wanted that car! My excitement began to grow when Dad said that we could afford it.

After my Dad signed the papers and made the purchase, we headed home. My Dad followed me in his car. As my hands gripped the steering wheel, I began to think about my grand entrance. You see, all of my buddies were playing basketball in my neighborhood. They would have front-row seats as I drove that sports car into my driveway for the first time. When they saw me cruise by, I would give them a grinning glance, followed by the cool man's chin nod. They would stop their basketball game and sprint over to my car, begging me for a ride through town.

As I pulled into the neighborhood, I slowed down. I wanted my buddies to catch a clear view of my sweet ride. When they saw me cruising by, they stopped their game. But their faces were expressing looks of utter confusion. After parking my sports car, I quickly got out. My friends were standing around me, shaking their heads. "What are those looks for?" I said. They just laughed at me and rolled their eyes. "You guys are just jealous of my new sports car," I proclaimed. "Sports car? That's not a sports car," one of my friends replied. "Of course it's a sports car!" I quickly responded. "No it's not…that is a Ford Tempo!" my friends shouted. And their laughter began.

You may be wondering why I thought a Ford Tempo was a sports car. Let me offer you two logical reasons. First of all, I was clueless about cars. After reading this brief story, this should not come as a surprise to you. Secondly, that Ford Tempo literally had the word 'Sport' painted on the doors! As laughter filled the air, my expectations experienced a head-on collision with reality. Ouch!

Expectations are powerful things. They can set us up for success or failure. When our expectations collide with reality, we can experience a major let down. But when our expectations align with reality, we can experience great joy. So it is important that we hold realistic expectations.

Are you carrying some false expectations in your marriage? Have you experienced some relational pain from previous collisions with reality? If so, you are not alone. Thousands of couples have walked down the aisle, expecting marriage to go a certain way. After the honeymoon phase is over, reality punches them like a heavy weight boxer.

We live in a world that tries to make everything in life easy. Think about this for a moment. If you are leaving work exhausted, you don't have to worry about cooking dinner. You can simply go through a drive-thru. Or lets say you are enjoying a day off and don't want to cook. You can order a pizza. And if you don't feel like talking to anybody, order the pizza online! When the delivery person knocks on your door, grab the pizza and cram some cash in the person's hand. You really don't have to say a word! Our society functions on the concept of making things easy. In fact, if something isn't easy, we probably won't pursue it.

Many couples enter marriage with similar expectations. They think that marriage should be easy. This false expectation sets them up for failure. When they begin to experience disagreements, the husband and wife can think that something is wrong with their marriage. In reality, there may not be anything wrong with their marriage. More than likely, the root of their problem rests in their expectations.

We must realize that God never intended marriage to be easy. God designed marriage to be holy. And holiness is never an easy road to travel. I want to challenge you to rethink some things. Romans 12:2 says, *"Do not conform any longer to the pattern of this world, but be transformed by the renewing of your mind."* As you read through the rest of this chapter, evaluate your mind. See if you are carrying some false expectations in your marriage. More than likely, you picked them up without even realizing it. False expectations can enter our minds through television, books, magazines, movies, music, advertisements, people, relationships and circumstances. They are all around us. Here are eight common false expectations men and women often carry into marriage.

1. **Intimacy Should Be Easy.**

We can thank the wide world of chick flicks for this one! Now ladies, put the cat claws away and hear me out on this one. There is nothing wrong with chick flicks in themselves. In fact, Melissa and I have enjoyed watching many together. Some of them have great story-lines. But we must recognize these movies are fantasy. Chick flicks do not reflect reality!

Although the names and faces change, every chick flick unfolds in similar ways. A guy and girl fall in love. Then they experience a conflict of some kind. The conflict stirs up strong emotions and they end up hurting each other's feelings. After separating from one another and pouting for a brief period of time, the couple will realize their love for one another. So they apologize and make out for a few moments. Then they live happily ever after.

Sadly, many couples expect their marriage to play out like a movie script. We think that intimacy should be easy. If we can find the 'right person' to marry then intimacy will naturally unfold. Although it may come easily during the early days of marriage, sustaining intimacy requires work.

Why is intimacy so difficult to sustain? James 3:2 says, *"We all stumble in many ways."* This little verse is packed with helpful truth. It provides realistic expectations for the road to marital intimacy. James is proclaiming that everybody sins. All of us will stumble! This means that it is only a matter of time before you say or do something that will hurt your spouse's feelings. And this will not be a one-time happening. For James says that everyone will "stumble in *many* ways."

So let's paint a realistic picture of intimacy in marriage. A husband who stumbles in many ways will marry a wife who stumbles in many ways. As they grow close with one another, they will find out that neither of them are perfect! We can be stubborn, cranky and hateful at times. Do you get the picture?

Intimacy is a free-will choice to live uncomfortably close with another imperfect person. True intimacy involves two imperfect people who are committed to living transparent lives together. They recognize their imperfections and make effort to grow. Intimacy requires work, sweat and unconditional commitment. Husbands and wives who successfully sustain intimacy understand this truth. There is nothing easy about it!

Although intimacy requires patience, work and sweat to sustain, it is well worth the time. You will gain a partner who will walk through the fires of conflict with you. And you will experience the joy of being close with someone who is always willing to forgive your faults. There will be no reason to hide from one another.

2. Sex will *always* be frequent.

Although husbands and wives can share this false expectation, men tend to carry this one the most. What would cause men to assume that high levels of sex will always exist in marriage? Pornography is a leading factor. Over the past twenty-five years, pornography has become widely accepted. It tops the charts as our countries leading money-maker. Although once sold in private places, it is now easily viewed from the internet. It has become accessible with the click of a mouse.

Pornography is fantasy. It portrays women as sexual objects who are always available for a good time. So countless husbands walk into marriage expecting their wife to play a role that doesn't exist! When their wives don't jump at every chance for sex, husbands feel rejected, and the wife feels hurt. She cannot compete with the fantasy roles of porn.

One of the fastest growing areas of the porn industry is women viewers. What is the reason for this increase in female viewers? Women have a thirst to be cherished. Many will even sacrifice their morals to have this thirst quenched. By viewing porn, women are making effort to learn what they think men are looking for. Women reason that if they can keep the attention and loyalty of their man, he will quench her thirst to be cherished. But immorality is never the answer. By imitating the things portrayed in pornography, a woman trades her true identity for a false image. So her man is not cherishing her. He is merely cherishing a false image of her.

Porn also feeds us lies about the purpose for sex. In the porn industry, sex is for pleasure. Through lustful encounters, men and women receive pleasure and then part ways. Sex is only a means of getting what you want. Intimacy is taken out of the equation.

Women are more than sexual toys! They are the daughters of God Almighty. They have been created with free will and are designed for more than the physical pleasure of men. It is important to understand this truth sooner than later. Husbands, expecting your wife to have sex whenever you want will cause major marriage problems. It will break her heart and be a source of ongoing frustration for you.

Let me give you an illustration that helps paint a picture of reality. If sex were water, men would be

Labrador retrievers and women would be camels. Men naturally crave sex more than women.

Our God has a great sense of humor! Understand that our differences are a good thing. If women desired sex as frequently as men, it would become all about the physical pleasure. Now this statement may sound appealing to men. But in reality, sex would become an empty act. We may be satisfied physically but our souls would thirst for more. Sex is more than physical pleasure! It is designed to bring husbands and wives into true intimacy. We'll talk about this more in a later chapter.

3. A husband is prince charming.

Little girls grow up thinking about the marriage ceremony. They often fantasize what their wedding day will be like and who their husband will be. Boyfriends are not simply someone to date or make out with. They may be their future hubby! This is why women put so much time, detail and sweat toward the wedding ceremony and reception. It is not just a day, it is The Day! They have been dreaming about this day for years.

Our culture is packed with fairy tale stories. They have been around for centuries. You know the picture. The princess has waited patiently for her knight to come into her life. When he arrives, he is riding a big white horse. Her knight comes fully loaded with poems, flowers, kind words of encouragement and table manners.

Now don't take me the wrong way. I am a huge fan of fairy tale stories! I'm a sucker for the action packed adventures and noble acts found within these tales. There is nothing wrong with enjoying a good fairy tale. And there is nothing wrong with a husband treating his wife like a queen. But we must realize that fairy tales are not reality.

During the honeymoon phase, husbands may appear to be a knight in shining armor. In reality, he is not. It is only a matter of time before he sticks his foot in his mouth. He will say stupid things that he doesn't really mean. He will act in selfish ways. He will burp, fart and smell badly at times. There will be moments when you experience his selective listening skills and stubborn will. When this reality collides with false expectations, wives often think *Who did I marry? I don't even know him! I didn't marry prince charming. I married prince chump!* In reality, he was never the knight in your dreams. He is a man.

4. Wives are sugar and spice and everything nice.

During the honeymoon phase, husbands often carry this false expectation. Wives seem so sweet. Their words are often affirming and supportive. Husbands can see their wives as innocent doves to care for. He believes she is made up of sugar and spice and everything nice. This false expectation is often planted by childhood nursery rhymes and chick flicks. Yes, ladies, chick flicks can affect the man's expectations, too.

This specific false expectation can grow through the "me too!" conversations in the dating years. Many men have experienced this in some way, shape or form. The man and woman go on a date. As they try to get to know one another, they share about their lives. During these early conversations, the woman can become overly agreeable.

Let me paint the picture for you. Jeff and Samantha are on their first date. The evening begins at a restaurant. As they eat their meal, they engage in conversation. Jeff shares about his passion for sports. Samantha seems to get excited. So Jeff narrows in on his favorite sport. "I really like football," he says. "Me too! I love football!" Samantha responds. Jeff suddenly feels like telling Samantha more details about his passion for football.

Now Samantha may actually like football. More than likely, she doesn't like the sport as much as Jeff. But they have experienced a relational connection. This connection feels good. As they continue in their conversation, Samantha may feel tempted to throw in some more "me too!" statements. As the temptation grows, she may even lie in order to feel the relational connection again.

Now Jeff is feeling a high level of respect from Samantha. She seems so supportive and affirming. As their feelings grow, they enjoy more dates. Eventually, Jeff proposes to Samantha and they get married. Life feels like a dream for them.

Things seem to be going well during the honeymoon phase. Samantha's "me too!" conversational pattern continues to some degree. After the honeymoon phase, things change. Samantha may not wear her make-up all the time or make effort to impress Jeff with her looks. Her words are not always encouraging either. Instead of constantly agreeing with Jeff's statements, Samantha shocks him with some argumentative remarks. She can come across as critical and disrespectful.

Samantha suddenly begins to remind Jeff of things. Some of her reminders come across as critical. Over time, Jeff begins to see her as a nag. Where did Jeff's sweet, innocent dove go?

When these moments enter a marriage, husbands often think *Who is she? How can such criticism come from such beautiful lips? Where did my fun-loving girlfriend go?* Men must realize that women are human, too. This means that they are not perfect. And they will not always agree with us!

5. If you marry your fiancé, your relational problems will go away.

I've seen this one play out in a variety of ways. After friends and family have been notified about the engagement, the couple feels obligated to push forward at all cost. Couples will often overlook major character flaws in the excitement of planning a wedding ceremony. Let me give you an example…

Peter and Jenny have been dating for about a year. Although they love each other, they have several topics of disagreement. Jenny hopes to have children but Peter does not like kids. Peter wants to move to another state in the next few years and travel the world. Jenny is close to her family and hopes to stay in the area. Jenny was raised in church and hopes that Peter will attend with her in the future. Peter doesn't seem interested in a relationship with Christ.

Six months ago, Peter popped the big question after a date night. It was a romantic moment and Jenny was totally taken by surprised. It took her breath away when Peter dropped to a knee. After a few moments of laughter and tears, Jenny emphatically said yes.

The past several months have been filled with a world of emotions. One moment they will be arguing and the next moment that will be hugging and kissing. Their friends have compared them to the leading characters from The Notebook. Always passionate, whether fighting or loving. As their wedding day approaches, each disagreement seems magnified. Both Peter and Jenny have some doubts about their engagement. Instead of talking about their doubts, they remain silent.

The day of the wedding finally arrives. Both Peter and Jenny place their disagreements aside. Jenny's bride's maids assure her that all the stress she feels is stemming from wedding preparations. Jenny expects smooth waters with Peter following the ceremony. Peter's best man tells him to focus on the honeymoon. Peter believes that everything will be ok once they get through the ceremony.

Couples often expect their fiancé to undergo positive change after the wedding day. They think that their vows will magically transform all of their relational struggles. In reality, their false expectations are setting them up for heart-ache.

6. Men and Women Are Equal

For several years, our society has been taught lies in the area of marriage, family and gender. Much confusion has been created! Have you ever heard the phrase, 'Men and women are equal'? At first glance, this statement seems true and even good. But it is a lie. Although men and women are equally loved and valued by God, we are not equal. If two or more objects are equal then they are the same. Think of these simple equations: 2 = 2, apples = apples and oranges = oranges. These equations are true. But you cannot mix them. Apples do not equal oranges. Even if you are a big fan of both apples and oranges, you still recognize the differences. The same is true with people. Man = Man and Woman = Woman. But Man does not equal Woman. We are not the same! Sadly, many of us have bought into our culture's lies.

When we enter marriage without understanding gender differences, we are setting ourselves up for frustration. If you want to experience a healthy marriage, recognize that men and women have been created in uniquely different ways. Turn to God's Word and embrace His design for your life. In a world of gender confusion, God's Word brings a breath of fresh air. Genesis 5:1 says, *"When God created man, He made him in the likeness of God. He created them male and female and blessed them."*

As men and women, we are both equally loved by our Creator. He blessed both genders! But He created us with differences. And this is a good thing! Instead of ignoring our gender differences or trying to manipulate them, we must embrace them.

7. Your spouse will complete you.

One of the problems with this false expectation is that it is so attracting. It seems to affirm your relationship and describe your spouse in a good way. When you embrace this expectation, you may even feel noble. But do not be deceived by its appearance.

This lie also makes mathematical sense. Think about this for a moment. $0.5 + 0.5 = 1$. This equation is true. But mathematical equations describe numbers, not human beings. When we try to use mathematical equations to describe marriage, we will cause more harm than good.

When we try to describe marriage with a mathematical equation, we use $0.5 + 0.5 = 1$. When we apply this equation to marriage, we are stating that two incomplete people (halves) become one complete person. Two halves equal one whole, right? In math, yes. But in marriage, no!

Genesis 2:24 says, "*For this reason a man will leave his father and mother and unite to his wife and the two will become one flesh.*" Notice the numbers in this verse. The two will become one. This verse is not describing mathematical addition. It is describing the blending of two lives.

When a husband and wife unite in marriage, two lives are blended together as one identity. We are no longer separate individuals. I am not only known as Seth. I am also known as Melissa's husband, and vice versa. The two lives have been blended into one.

So let's keep the mathematical equations where they belong. Let them describe numbers. But do not allow them to describe marriage!

8. Romance will never fade.

This lie is one of the most common that couples believe. We naturally pick it up from the romantic culture that we live in. Movies, television shows, commercials, books, magazines and music is saturated with romance. It is all around us! Now there is nothing evil about romance in itself. The trouble comes when we believe that it is supposed to last forever.

I remember carrying this lie myself. During our dating years, Melissa and I experienced the butterflies of romance. It was great! We would notice older couples from time to time. You know the ones I am talking about. The ones who never hold hands or show any form of public affection. My natural reaction to these couples was very judgmental. "That will never be us!" I would proclaim. In my mind, something was terribly wrong with a couple who did not express high levels of romance.

I can remember talking about this topic with an elderly lady at our home church. As I shared about the perfection of my romantic relationship with Melissa, this lady demonstrated high levels of patience. "I refuse to allow the butterflies to leave my relationship with Melissa!" I said. Then I shared my opinion that romance should never fade. I honestly thought that if the butterfly-like feelings left, there would be something wrong in my relationship with Melissa.

This lady eventually shared truth with me. "Seth, I love my husband and we have been married over thirty-five years." she gently said. "Do you still feel butterflies when you look at him?" I asked. "Sometimes I do. But not all the time," she continued. I remember thinking that she must be experiencing some marriage problems. As she continued to explain her answer, my ears gained a gold-mine of truth. "The butterflies never stay, Seth. But they will always come back. My job is to have my heart prepared to receive them," she explained.

What a powerful truth! Although I didn't fully comprehend what she was saying at the time, her words planted a seed of truth in my mind. Romance is like a butterfly. Your heart is like a flower. The butterfly often flutters here and there, resting for brief moments in time as it drinks from a flower. Just like the butterfly, romance was not created to stay in one spot for eternity. And just like the flower, our hearts must be prepared to receive romance during those awesome moments when it returns.

Overcoming False Expectations

Have you experienced any of these false expectations? Perhaps you have. Or maybe you have been carrying different ones. These eight false expectations are not an exhaustive list. They are simply the ones I've heard and experienced most.

False expectations always set marriages up for relational stress. If you have been carrying false expectations in your marriage, you must rethink things. You may be tempted to hold on to your false expectations or force your spouse to conform to them. But this will never work! It may be difficult to let them go. For you may have been carrying them in your mind for years. But you must let them go. Get rid of them! You'll be glad that you did. You'll be freeing up your mind to accept God's expectations for marriage.

This leads us to an important question. What are God's expectations for marriage? What does He expect from husbands and wives? I can sum this question up in one word: holiness. A holy marriage is consecrated, set apart from the ways of this world. A holy marriage functions the way God designed marriage to be. And a holy marriage works! Perhaps an even greater question must be asked. What does a holy marriage look like? I'll answer that in the next chapter. Before moving to the next chapter, prepare your mind. Follow God's guidance in the following verse. Then you will be able to see God's wonderful plan for your marriage.

"Do not conform any longer to the pattern of this world, but be transformed by the renewing of your mind. Then you will be able to test and approve what God's will is-His good, pleasing and perfect will." - Romans 12:2

Biblical Roles of Husband & Wife

"Submit to one another out of reverence for Christ."

- Ephesians 5:21

"Each one of you also must love his wife as he loves himself, and the wife must respect her husband."
- Ephesians 5:33

This morning, I woke up with Cinnamon Apple Spice hot tea on my mind. The season of fall brings on this craving within me. So I stopped by a local grocery store on my way to the office. Finding the tea was no problem, for I knew the aisle of its location.

After grabbing a box, I made my way to the check-out lanes. I was the only customer checking out at the time so I was thinking this may be a world record for the quickest errand! Only one lane had its light on, signaling that it was open for business. After walking into the lane, I stood there to pay.

For some reason, nobody was stationed at the cash register. I looked to my right and noticed an employee cleaning another register area. Then I looked to my left and saw another employee accomplishing a similar task. My eyes then glanced to make sure the light for my lane was on. Yes, it was on! So I simply looked toward both of the employees as they cleaned. When they noticed me, both seemed to be confused. They were both intensely focused on their cleaning tasks and struggled to break away. It was funny to watch them stare at one another for a moment. They were trying to figure out who was responsible for helping me! Thankfully, one of them stepped up.

It's always important to understand your role and responsibilities in life. This is true for the workplace and at home. Based on the current divorce rate, many husbands and wives are living in confusion. One of my favorite questions to ask couples is '*What is your God-given role in your marriage?*' I often get a blank stare and the sound of crickets. The silence is normally broken by hesitant answers as the couple hopes to get one of their answers right.

Understanding God's design for husbands and wives is crucial for achieving a healthy marriage. God has created our specific roles and we must understand them. Then we can seize our responsibility and grow as husbands and wives. Husband, do you understand your God-given role in your marriage? Wife, do you understand your God-given role in your marriage? This chapter will provide solid answers for you.

Mutual Submission

Ephesians 5:21 says, *"Submit to one another out of reverence for Christ."* This is a goldmine of truth for husbands and wives! For years, Christians have overlooked the power in this verse. Christian couples have heard countless sermons commanding wives to submit to their husbands. Although these sermons are biblical, they are often incomplete. These sermons tend to paint one side of the picture. For submission in marriage is a two way street.

Paul is commanding both husbands and wives to submit to one another. Some of you may be thinking, *But Seth, I thought the husband was supposed to be the leader of the home!* Understand that this verse is not talking about leadership. That topic is covered in the following verses. Paul is commanding both husbands and wives to submit to one another's needs at all cost. This is a high calling and requires much sacrifice. The husband must submit to meeting his wife's needs and the wife must submit to meeting her husband's needs.

As a husband and wife enter marriage, their individual identities must die. Before marriage, the husband and wife were individuals. They had their own agendas and goals. In marriage, the two have become one flesh. This means that the husband and wife must leave their individual lives and walk together as one. The marriage relationship must be a higher priority than individual agendas. In marriage, the focus must become 'we' instead of 'me.' Ephesians 5:31 says, *"For this reason, a man will leave his father and mother and will unite to his wife, and the two will become one flesh."* Paul is quoting God's design for marriage from Genesis

2:24. When God's Word repeats the same verse, it must be important!

Paul also addresses the correct motivation for meeting your spouse's needs. He says that we must mutually submit to one another "*out of reverence for Christ.*" Our primary motivation for meeting one another's needs must stem from our devotion to Jesus Christ. Your willingness to meet the needs of your spouse is directly proportionate to your reverence for Christ. This means that if you are struggling to meet the needs of your spouse, your primary problem does not rest in your marriage. Your problem is coming from something hindering your relationship with Christ. In order to fully meet your spouse's needs, you must walk in reverence to Jesus Christ daily.

What would cause Paul to draw this connection? There will be times that you feel like meeting the needs of your spouse. And there will be moments when you do not feel like doing so. Our culture teaches that we must trust our feelings and operate from them. But feelings come and go. Feelings cannot always be trusted. What we need is a solid motivation that empowers us to provide for one another's needs. Jesus Christ is the One who can empower us to meet one another's needs and desire to do so. You cannot fully meet one another's needs without Him!

Now that we have covered the concept of mutual submission, we can address the God-given roles for husbands and wives. So what is the role of a husband?

What role does a wife play in marriage? In order to walk together as one flesh, we must be able to answer these questions.

The roles for husbands and wives are to serve as the primary care-givers within the marriage relationship. The husband must meet his wife's needs and the wife must meet her husband's needs. In order to meet one another's needs, we must fully understand them.

Ephesians 5:33 says, *"Each one of you (husbands) must love his wife as he loves himself and the wife must respect her husband."* The primary need of a man is respect and the primary need of a woman is to feel cherished. God wants to use husbands and wives to meet one another's needs!

Men, let this truth sink in for a moment. The primary need of your wife is to feel cherished, and the Creator of this Universe wants to use you to meet that need! This is one of the most significant things you will ever accomplish in this world. Listen carefully to God's call for you as a husband. *"Each of you must love his wife as he loves himself."* One of the key words in this verse is *'must'*. It means that it has to happen. There are no loop holes here! You must meet your wife's need to feel cherished, no matter what. Her need must be met unconditionally. There will be times you feel like she deserves to be cherished, and there will be times when she may not deserve it. In this area of marriage, the word 'deserve' does not even apply. Her need to feel cherished must be met unconditionally, no matter how you feel in a particular moment.

Ladies, the primary need of a man is to feel respect. I know what some of you may be thinking. *Seth, that doesn't make sense to me! I thought the primary need of men is to feel loved. Everybody needs to feel loved!* I agree with you. But you must understand how God has wired your man. The universal love language of men is respect. If you don't believe me, try this. Ask your husband if he would rather hear the words 'I love you' or 'I really respect you.' He will choose the latter!

Ephesians 5:33 says, *"The wife must respect her husband."* Your expression of respect must be unconditional. This truth can be extremely difficult for wives to obey, especially when there are problems in a marriage. In most areas of life, respect must be earned, and rightly so. It is never wise to respect someone you do not know! But in marriage, you already know your husband. God wants to use you to meet your husband's need to feel respected. This need must be met, whether you think he deserves it or not.

The Insanity Cycle

What happens when husbands and wives neglect to meet one another's needs? What happens when a wife refuses to respect her hubby? What happens when a husband does not meet his wife's need to feel cherished? They will enter something I call The Insanity Cycle.

A wise man once defined insanity as doing the same thing over and over again, expecting different results. When a husband does not meet his wife's need to feel cherished, she feels neglected. Her response will be disrespect toward her husband. She may come across as nagging and critical toward his thoughts and opinions. Her words will tear him down, rather than build him up. If the wife does not feel cherished by her husband, she will be tempted to seek alternate ways for being cherished outside the marriage.

When a wife does not meet her hubby's need for respect, he will lash out in unloving ways. His ears will be closed to intimate conversations with her. Instead of holding her hand or putting his arm around her, she will experience a cold shoulder. Instead of cherishing her company, he will either avoid her or treat her like an opponent. Men will often spend excessive amounts of time at work or with friends. Men tend to go where the cheers are.

Here is what is insane about this cycle. The wife wants to feel cherished. And the husband wants to feel respected. Both are pointing fingers to the faults of their spouse, while neither of them are having their needs met! The husband will never get respect while he continues to act unloving toward his wife. The wife will never feel cherished while lashing out in disrespectful ways. This is insanity!

When couples are doing life in The Insanity Cycle, they are blind to their own faults. Their eyes are pointing out the other person's inability to meet their needs. Christ addressed this tendency in Matthew 7:3-5. Christ said, *"Why do you look at the speck of sawdust in your brother's eyes and pay no attention to the plank in your own eye? How can you say to your brother, 'Let me take the speck out of your eye', when all the time there is a plank in your own eye? You hypocrite, first take the plank out of your own eye..."* Ouch. Sometimes the truth can humble us. This is a good thing.

Let's be honest for a moment. There is no such thing as a perfect marriage. Remember that James 3:2 says, *"We all stumble in many ways."* This means that every marriage will enter The Insanity Cycle from time to time. But the key is to recognize it as early as possible. There will be times when the husband will recognize The Insanity Cycle first. There will be other times that the wife will. Once you recognize it, stop the insanity! Look at your spouse and say, "This is insane! We are experiencing The Insanity Cycle!"

After you recognize The Insanity Cycle, take responsibility for your words and actions. Husband, ask your wife, "What did I say or do to make you feel unloved?" Wife, ask your husband, "What did I say or do to make you feel disrespected?" Listen to one another's pain. There is great power when our pain is heard. By listening, you will be showing that you care.

As you listen and talk with your spouse, confess your sins to one another. James 5:16 says, *"Therefore confess your sins to each other and pray for each other so you may be healed.*" By confessing your sins, you may find healing for your heart. As you both confess your sins, forgive one another. Release your anger and resentment. This will bring reconciliation to your marriage.

Perhaps you have been living in The Insanity Cycle for a good while now. If so, you may find it difficult to forgive your spouse. You may also be dealing with issues of broken trust. If you are struggling to break free from The Insanity Cycle, seek help. Contact your pastor, a Christian counselor or a friend who can help you follow Christ's path of reconciliation. Your marriage is worth it! Whoever you choose, make sure they are walking with Christ and will offer you wise counsel. You also need to make sure that your spouse affirms the person you go to for help.

Planning To Grow Together

When couples contact me for biblical marriage counsel, I know what to expect out of our first meeting. Although the faces and names change, things tend to play out in the following way…

The couple will sit down in my office. Their body language reflects their frustrations. The wife often leans away from her husband and the husband normally sits with his arms crossed. Although they scheduled this appointment, they do not look happy about being here.

I kick things off by giving them realistic expectations. I explain that we will not solve all of their problems in this one meeting and the couple is challenged to persevere. Then I explain that the purpose for the first meeting is for them to share specific areas of their relationship that require change. At this point, we experience some awkward silence while the couple decides who will go first.

Normally the wife kicks things off. After she highlights multiple faults in her husband, he is motivated to fight back. Have you ever witnessed a two-liter coke being opened after someone has shaken it up? That's what happens in my office! Suddenly the couple is arguing, bringing up unresolved disagreements, pet-peeves and the like. It looks like an adult version of the childhood game King of the Hill.

What do I do? I watch, listen and pray for God to show me the right time to speak. What do they want me to do? Jump in and take sides. They want me to be their marriage referee. So I explain that I'm not going to choose to be on either of their sides. I'm on God's side.

I ask them if they would like to know what God expects from them. They say that they do, reluctantly. So I take them to Ephesians 5:33 and read it. *"Each one of you must love his wife as he loves himself and the wife must respect her husband."* Silence. I explain to the husband that he must cherish his wife. Then I explain to the wife that she must respect her husband. Both love and respect must be unconditional.

I look at the husband and ask, "Do you cherish your wife?" He quickly responds with a "yes." So I ask the

wife if she respects her husband and she says "yes."
Then I ask the husband, "Do you believe that she respects
you?" He proclaims, "No!" I then ask the wife if she
believes that her husband cherishes her. She quickly
replies, "No!" The couple faces a major obstacle.
Although they claim to feel love and respect for their
spouse, they accuse the other person of lying. The wife
asks, "When do you cherish me?" The husband
asks, "When do you respect me?"

When couples enter The Insanity Cycle, they often
claim to cherish and respect one another. I rarely
question their feelings toward one another. The
confusion comes from their expression. Although a
husband may cherish his wife, his expression must back
it up. If a wife truly respects her husband, then her
expression of respect must prove it. Husband, does your
wife believe that you cherish her with all of your heart?
Wife, does your husband believe that you respect him
unconditionally? How effective is your expression?
Understand that your expression will determine your
effectiveness in meeting your spouse's needs.

Wife, how can you grow in meeting your hubby's
need to feel respect? Men, how can you grow in helping
your wife feel more cherished? Ask your spouse! Don't
make assumptions. For you know what they say about
assumptions. When I assume something, I'm only
making a....donkey out of you and me. You know what
I'm saying here....

Here is a great exercise to go through with your spouse. It will promote growth in your effectiveness to meet each other's needs. Sit down and talk. Listen to one another. You may be surprised by what you learn.

- Husband, ask your wife to give you 3-5 things you can say or do that will help her feel cherished by you.

- Wife, ask your husband to give you 3-5 things you can say or do that will help him feel respected by you.

I remember a time when Melissa and I went through this exercise. Honestly, I thought I was doing a great job in making her feel cherished! We had been together for several years. So I was expecting her to say things like "Seth, I would feel more cherished if you would get me more flowers or write more poems." Her answers caught me by surprise. She said things like, "Seth, If you get to bed first, I would feel more cherished if you would fold down the cover and sheets on my side of the bed for me." *What?* I would have never predicted an answer like that! I was able to learn more about Melissa and how to make her feel more cherished.

Every person is uniquely made by God. No two people are the same. So we must avoid making gender-specific assumptions. Some women like flowers and some do not. Some men like sports magazines and some do not. If you want to meet the needs of your spouse, ask them how.

Husband, cherish your wife! Wife, respect your husband! God wants to use you both to meet one another's needs. What a wonderful responsibility God has given us. May our reverence for Him serve as our underlining motivation. And may we be faithful in our roles as husbands and wives.

Open Communication

"Do not let any unwholesome talk come out of your mouths, but only what is helpful for building others up according to their needs, that it may benefit those who listen." - Ephesians 4:29

Imagine that you are in your favorite restaurant. Try to picture it in your mind. The sights and smells are familiar to you. You already know what you will order before you look at the menu. In fact, the only reason you look at the menu is to glance at something until your server comes back with your drink. As the server brings your drink, you place your food order. The communication is kind, yet brief and to the point.

Now you wait. To help pass the time, you glance around the restaurant. Your eyes begin to look at the pictures on the walls and the other decorations. You take mental notes of the details you didn't notice as you were rushed to your seat. Then you quickly check your cell phone for texts, emails or other alerts. As you continue to wait, you begin to notice the other people dining around you. *Who are these people? What is their story in life? What do they do for a living?* You begin to wonder.

We've heard the age-old proverbial glass illustration. If you were to ask each of these people about their proverbial glass in life, most would claim they see it as half full. The reason for their response is simple. Most people have the desire to be positive. Nobody wants to focus on the negative parts of life! What's the alternative for half full? Half empty. These two words seem so negative, so demeaning. Nobody wants these words to describe their life. So we cover them up with positive words. Half full. Now that has a better ring to it! But if you would follow each of these people on any given day, you may be shocked by what you find. Although they claim to see their proverbial glass in life as half full, they are living as if it is half empty. Their lives contradict their words. What about you? If you were asked about your proverbial glass in life, how would you respond? Would your answer line up with your lifestyle?

Too many husbands and wives are settling in their marriage. They would likely define their relationship as half full. But if you walked with them throughout the day, you would see a contradiction. It looks like they are settling for something less than they signed up for. They wouldn't claim to be living at rock bottom. For they know countless couples facing a crisis of some kind.

Things could definitely be worse for them. They breathe a sigh of relief. At least their relationship isn't as bad as 'so-and-so's' marriage.

My Problem With The Proverbial Glass

I cannot count the number of times I've heard the proverbial glass illustration, and even used it myself. The more I hear it, something stirs within me. You see, it has a major fault. To be honest with you, I don't like either option the illustration gives! The half empty option is obviously negative. In fact, it is extremely negative. When you compare this option with the second, being half full, the latter seems positive. But think about this for a moment. If someone asked you what you want out of life, would you really want to be half full? Would you choose to have these words describe your marriage? Would you choose these words to be spoken at your funeral or etched on your tombstone?

Half full. These words seem to fall short. They describe something that didn't quite meet expectations, for whatever reason. They imply that the greatest potential was not met. If these words were applied to a school report card, you would be looking at all C's. If they were applied to a sporting event, you would be facing a tie with the other team. Remember that old saying about ties? Nobody wants to kiss their sister! If these words were applied to a fast-food meal, the fries would be cold. If these words describe your career, your boss and coworkers would think you are holding back. If they were applied to a marriage, people would confess that they settled.

What is the secret to a great marriage? What is one of the most important topics for husbands and wives to address? One of the ingredients to a great marriage rests in communication. Communication affects all areas of marriage. You cannot get away from it! Finances, sex, intimacy, parenting, hobbies, values, shopping, vacations, balancing family and your career, time management, dealing with in-laws and conflict all require communication. Your ability to communicate effectively will determine how healthy or unhealthy your marriage will be.

Couples who experience a great marriage intentionally work on their communication. They refuse to settle for a marriage that is half empty or half full. Deep down, they sense that God has something more for them to experience. So they commit to chase after God's best.

What does it take to have open communication in marriage? Let me share seven steps that will help you get there. As you read though them, highlight your strengths and weaknesses.

1. Be Truth-Full

It is important to be honest with your spouse, all the time! I know what some of you guys are thinking. *Ok, Seth, lets say my wife has put on a few pounds since our wedding day. Then she approaches me and asks if she looks fat in a particular outfit. What do I say?* Most husbands have been in a similar situation. So I say be prepared! Work on your delivery of truth. How you say something is as important as what you say. But lying is never the answer! How can we expect God to bless our marriage if we cannot speak the truth?

God wants husbands and wives to speak the truth to one another. If you are struggling to be honest with your spouse, your problem may rest in the area of fear. Think about it. Most people lie because they fear something. Children lie because they don't want to get in trouble. Adults do the same thing. If you find yourself struggling to be truthful with your spouse, meditate on this verse. 1 John 4:18 says, *"There is no fear in love but perfect love drives out fear."* What are you afraid of? Don't let that fear hold you back from speaking the truth. It is impossible for fear and love to coexist in the heart! Address your fear. Share it openly with your spouse. And start walking in the way of truth.

2. Be An Active Listener

Most people are selective listeners. We simply listen in order to formulate a response. Once we gain enough information to form a response, we begin rehearsing it in our mind. We are all guilty of this!

Active listening is different. Active listening seeks to understand the other person. The goal is to understand your spouse, not to simply respond to their words. Proverbs 18:13 says, *"He who answers before listening—that is his folly and shame."* God wants husbands and wives to move beyond the surface level of communication. He wants us to truly get to know one another. So we must choose to grow as active listeners rather than living as selective listeners.

3. Be Transparent

Most men have found themselves in the following scenario. You are enjoying an evening with your wife. Dinner was delicious and now you are watching a movie. Since you are hoping to make-out later in the evening, you agree to watch a chick flick. Your wife thinks you are tender hearted, but your decision was an act of fore-play!

At some point during the evening, your wife decides to ask you the dreaded question. *What are you thinking about?* Wives, this little question takes men off guard.

The wife is actually inviting her husband to be transparent. The husband views it as some type of trick question. He normally responds with, "Uh….I love you?"

Being transparent can be especially difficult for men. Men grow up being told that they must be strong and brave. Weaknesses are not to be openly discussed. So men try to hide their weaknesses, thinking that their wife doesn't need to know. They feel vulnerable discussing topics that reveal personal shortcomings.

A wife can also struggle to be open with their husband. Perhaps she was rejected in a previous relationship, or she may be carrying pain from a past boyfriend or husband. Proverbs 4:23 says, *"Above all else, guard your heart for it is the wellspring of life."* Everything we say or do flows from the heart. And if there is pain present, we need to address it.

If you want to experience open communication in marriage, you must seek to be transparent with one another! Being transparent isn't easy, but it is worth the effort. So push through any obstacle that may be keeping you from sharing all areas of life together.

4. Be Grace-Full

People who extend grace to others are a joy to be around! They help people feel at ease. Extending grace is an open invitation to address past, present and future sins. It empowers couples to experience reconciliation after a disagreement and opens the door to the beautiful exchange of *'I'm sorry'* and *'I forgive you'*.

When a marriage lacks grace, the husband and wife will become defensive toward one another. They will feel the need to justify themselves and point blame in another direction. Husbands and wives will fail to accept responsibility for their words and actions. The blame game blocks opportunities for growth during conflict.

Let's be honest. There is no such thing as a perfect husband or wife! Grace frees us from trying to be something we are not. It helps us find true acceptance in our marriage. Colossians 4:6 says, *"Let your conversation be always full of grace."* Grace empowers us to accept and extend forgiveness when needed. It is God's gift that can hold a marriage together through the difficult seasons.

5. Be Up-lifting

Most of us grew up under the influence of a deadly nursery rhyme. You fill in the blank here. "Sticks and stones may break my bones but words

_____ " Words may never hurt me. What a lie! In reality, words are powerful. Proverbs 18:21 says, *"The tongue has the power of life and*

death…" Our tongues hold the power to encourage our spouse in ways that nobody else can. Our tongues can also pierce the heart of the one we love most.

I was recently talking with a good friend. We were discussing God's design for marriage. As we talked, we exchanged stories of how our wives have encouraged us. I loved the conclusion of our conversation. *"My wife empowers me to be the best husband I can possibly be!"* we both proclaimed in agreement.

A few weeks ago, I hit writer's block. The faucet of creativity instantly shut off in my mind. As I stared at my computer screen, I wondered how in the world I would finish that specific chapter. The silence was broken by my cell phone as it signaled that I received a text message. The text message was from Melissa. It simply read *"I love you. You are a great writer!"* That simple text message empowered me to overcome writer's block. The creativity began to flow as my office was filled once again, with the sound of typing.

Couples who experience open communication understand the importance of encouragement. An encouraging word goes a long way! So use your words to lift your spouse up. Follow the wisdom in the book of Ephesians. Ephesians 4:29 says, *"Do not let any unwholesome talk come out of your mouths, but only what is helpful for building others up according to their needs, that it may benefit those who listen."*

6. Handle Your Anger Biblically

Ephesians 4:26-27 says, *"In your anger do not sin. Do not let the sun go down while you are still angry, and do not give the devil a foothold."* There is so much wisdom in these verses! Anger is a powerful emotion. It can easily lead us toward sinful behavior. Most people tend to deal with anger in one of two ways. We either explode in the moment or hold everything inside. Neither responses are biblical, and both hinder our communication in marriage.

When I was a bachelor, I did some stupid things. I once had a gallon of milk that had expired in my refrigerator. Instead of throwing it away, I decided to turn it into a little experiment. That milk sat in my refrigerator for several months.

One hot summer morning, I decided to dispose of that milk. So I sat the jug in my backyard. Throughout the day, the sun beat down upon the milk and the jug expanded. When I came home from work, I shot the milk jug with my gun. It made a loud pop and began to ooze the expired milk all over the lawn. The milk looked like cottage cheese, but it smelled like road-kill! I was gagging while I cleaned the mess up! What would cause a guy to do something like this? Contrary to popular belief, bachelors are not always deep thinkers. I didn't think through things. My decision was simply based on the thought of shooting a milk jug with a gun.

Anger can be like spoiled milk. It needs to be disposed of quickly and properly. When anger is expressed in unbridled ways, it can make a mess of things. When we bottle it up, anger will rot us from the inside out. When it is exposed, it can be nasty. So we must deal with our anger biblically! Tell your spouse about your anger. And use wisdom as you express it.

7. Be Giving

This may come as a surprise, but you and your spouse will not always agree. Now it is important to walk in full agreement on the big things in life. What are the big things in life? These are things that have eternal significance. The big things would be matters of faith, parenting, where we live, where we go to church, our career path, balancing work and family, serving Christ and sex. Ok, I only threw sex in there to make sure the men were still paying attention.

I'm amazed by how we can make mountains out of mole hills. We can take non-moral issues and treat them like matters of salvation. It is important to keep the big things the big things and keep the small things the small things. Holding the right perspective is important. We will address how to approach the big things in the following chapter. Right now, we'll focus on how to handle a disagreement over something small.

Husbands and wives must be willing to compromise in areas that hold no eternal value. What color will you paint the house? What will you watch on television this evening? Where will your family go on vacation? Who will you spend the holidays with? What kind of car will you purchase? What should you wear to church? Who should make the bed in the mornings? Don't be petty! 1 Corinthians 16:14 says, *"Do everything in love."* Be willing to compromise on the small things. It communicates the fact that your spouse is more important than your opinion.

If you desire open communication, you must be willing to give toward the greater good of your spouse. This means that there will be some areas of compromise. Remember that the purpose for marriage is not to get what you want. The purpose for marriage is to walk as one flesh. So be giving!

Which of these seven steps are you currently practicing in your marriage? Which of these steps do you need to work on? Start working on these steps today! Sit down with your spouse and make a plan. Grab your calendar and mark off the next seven days. Choose one of the steps to work on daily. Start talking and listening. Be patient with one another. Don't settle for a marriage that is half empty or half full. Reach for a full marriage! Change is within your reach.

Removing Relational Walls

"Let love and faithfulness never leave you. Bind them around your neck. Write them on the tablet of your heart." - Proverbs 3:3

When I was growing up, some of my neighbors had a disagreement. Although I didn't know what caused it, I could clearly see the effects. Their arguments often grew into shouting competitions. It was an ugly sight for a little boy to see! I can remember thinking, *Why can't my neighbors get along?* In a matter of days, our neighborhood was aware of the disagreement. If you were to visit one of these feuding neighbors, they would make the other out to be the devil.

As things progressed, my neighbors became extremely territorial. They clearly marked the boundary line between their lawns. It looked like two toddlers shouting "Mine! Mine! Mine!" Both understood that the other neighbor would be trespassing if they dared to cross the property line. One of them even made threats to call the police if the other chose to trespass.

This disagreement continued over the span of several months. Although each neighbor was kind to others, they would intentionally give each other the cold shoulder. Finally, one of the feuding neighbors decided the boundary line was not enough separation. So he built a tall wooden fence. The fence made the statement, "Ha! Take that! Now I don't even have to look at you!"

From that point on, the fence stood as a lasting symbol of separation. It proclaimed, "We will never reconcile our disagreement!" In the sixteen years of living in that neighborhood, I didn't see the fence come down. Although the intense anger seemed to go away, the separation remained. That fence became a relational wall between my neighbors. Their hearts continued to grow cold toward one another over the years.

We can face similar situations in marriage. God's design for marriage is for husbands and wives to live as one flesh. Although countless husbands and wives agree with God's design, few will live it out. The concept of living as one flesh is easy to understand but much harder to follow on a consistent basis.

What makes living as one flesh so difficult? Living as one flesh involves two separate people with individual perspectives coming together as one. Throughout the years of living as individuals, we develop habits, both in behavior and thought patterns. We are used to living and viewing life a particular way. As we enter marriage, our perspectives will experience collisions at times. We will not see life through the exact same lens! As disagreements arise, our tendency is to pull away.

More than likely, you've heard the phrase '*We must agree to disagree.*' The purpose is to keep peace with others. This mentality seems to work well in many circumstances. For it allows us to keep the main thing the main thing. What is the main thing? Peace! This phrase can keep peace in friendships and in the workplace.

For example, by agreeing to disagree about certain matters, employees can keep peace within the workplace. Employees don't have to like each other. They can simply agree to keep peace for eight hours a day and cooperate. Their eyes focus on the tasks at hand. But this is only temporary peace. It only exists during specific hours of the day. When an employee clocks out, they don't have to go home with employees they don't like!

So agreeing to disagree can benefit many areas of life. But this phrase was never intended to be practiced in marriage. Marriage is the only relationship with the purpose of living as one flesh. Many husbands and wives walk into marriage with the pattern of keeping temporary peace. So they will approach matters of disagreement with this intention.

When marital disagreements arise, many couples will simply agree to disagree. But 'agreeing to disagree' does not work in marriage. Husbands and wives do not clock in or clock out of marriage. They must live together! When husbands and wives agree to disagree, they are actually building relational walls into their marriage. What is a relational wall? A relational wall is anything that prevents a husband and wife from experiencing oneness. Walls are often built through disagreements.

Here are some common relational walls that couples face. As you read through them, highlight the one(s) that exist in your marriage. In order for you to experience oneness with your spouse, you must recognize your relational walls.

- In-Laws

- The Process of Blending Families

- Parenting

- Neglect

- Priority Differences

- Sexual Expectations

- Finances

- Time Management

- Pain From Past Relationships

Which of these relational walls exist in your marriage? After recognizing your wall(s), you must plan to remove it. Husbands and wives must intentionally work together to remove each one. Now you may be thinking that your relational walls aren't really that big of a deal. And you may be thinking that agreeing to disagree has been working well for you. Let me show you how relational walls affect marriages over time.

During the early years of marriage, husbands and wives can experience high levels of romantic feelings. When a couple recognizes a topic of disagreement, they often agree to disagree. By doing so, they build a wall around that particular topic and avoid discussing it again. They simply lock that topic away in a "Do Not Enter" zone. This doesn't seem to affect the marriage early on. They are still in the process of getting to know one another. They still have a world of topics they can discuss! So it is easy to avoid that one area of disagreement.

In time, the husband and wife will discover more topics of disagreement. If they continue practicing the method of agreeing to disagree, they will continue building walls around those topics. As this pattern continues, they will find themselves with fewer topics to discuss. So their communication will become less and less. Eventually, they will struggle to have conversation. As more walls have been built over time, the damage will be evident. The husband and wife will feel awkward around each other.

Relational walls separate husbands and wives! It is impossible to experience oneness with your spouse while living with relational walls. The passion of romance will fade and your hearts will grow cold. When hearts grow cold, they can become hardened. Matthew 19 addresses the danger of a hardened heart. Read verses 1-9 below.

When Jesus had finished saying these things, he left Galilee and went into the region of Judea to the other side of the Jordan. Large crowds followed him, and he healed them there. Some Pharisees came to him to test him. They asked, "Is it lawful for a man to divorce his wife for any and every reason?" "Haven't you read," he replied, "that at the beginning the Creator 'made them male and female,' and said, 'For this reason a man will leave his father and mother and be united to his wife, and the two will become one flesh'? So they are no longer two, but one. Therefore what God has joined together, let man not separate." "Why then," they asked, "did Moses command that a man give his wife a certificate of divorce

and send her away?" Jesus replied, "Moses permitted
you to divorce your wives because your hearts were hard.
But it was not this way from the beginning. I tell you that
anyone who divorces his wife, except for marital
unfaithfulness, and marries another woman commits
adultery."

In this passage, Jesus addresses the leading cause for divorce. Some people think that the leading causes for divorce would be things like broken trust, cheating, lying or abuse. Although these are all serious issues, they are only symptoms of something far worse. The number one cause for divorce is a hardened heart. When a spouse develops a hardened heart, they are in deadly territory. They will do things to their spouse they swore they would never do.

How do husbands and wives develop a hardened heart toward one another? They slowly develop hardened hearts by constructing relational walls. Relational walls hinder God's design for a one flesh marriage. It is impossible to experience ongoing oneness with your spouse with the existence of relational walls. At best, you will settle for a counterfeit form of peace. At worst, you will develop a hardened heart and begin taking steps down the road of divorce. So let's remove those relational walls! Here are some helpful steps to take…

1. **Be devoted to your spouse for life.** Proverbs 3:3 says, *"Let love and faithfulness never leave you. Bind them around your neck and write them on the tablet of*

your heart." You must develop a "Never Give Up" mentality! Be devoted to walk with your spouse for better or for worse. Place your marriage as a higher priority than pet-peeves. Any relational wall can be conquered by a husband and wife who are truly devoted to one another.

2. **Understand Your Perspectives**. By talking through a disagreement, you will be able to understand yourself and your spouse's perspective. Most people rarely take the time to understand their own perspective! They simply assume they are right and make great effort to defend their position. It is also important to understand your spouse's perspective. Listen and try to understand. More than likely, you will both learn something!

3. **Persevere Through Disagreements.** James 5:11 says, *"We consider blessed those who have persevered."* One of my good friends recently had a disagreement with his wife. Due to the economy, they were experiencing some financial stress with some real estate property they own. Whenever the topic came up, they would express different solutions to the problem. They couldn't seem to find a mutual agreement. But they didn't give up! My friends would take a break from discussing it with the intent of bringing up the matter at a later time. Many couples would simply agree to disagree. But my friends persevered. By doing so, they eventually found a solution they both could commit to. Their perseverance was worth it!

4. **Seek Wise Counsel**. Proverbs 13:20 says, *"He who walks with the wise grows wise."* It is important for both you and your spouse to have someone wise that you may turn to. An outside perspective can really help shed Christ's light on things. When we disagree with our spouse, it's easy to gain tunnel vision. We often see our disagreement from our own perspective. Wise counsel helps bring us back to reality. Our eyes gain a clear perspective of reality. We are empowered to see the bigger picture.

   As you seek wise counsel, make sure that you choose someone who is not afraid to speak truth into your life. Your wise counsel may come from another Christian couple who can meet with you at the same time. Or you may find wise counsel individually.

   It is important for your spouse to feel comfortable with whoever you turn to for counsel. It is also important for you to establish boundaries. What is ok for you to discuss with this person? What is not ok to discuss? Setting those boundaries will help keep your marriage away from areas of broken trust.

5. **Be Patient**. Proverbs 16:32 says, *"Better a patient man than a warrior, a man who controls his temper than one who takes a city."* Removing a relational wall may not happen over-night. Sometimes it takes days, weeks or even months. As you walk through the process of removing a wall, be patient with your spouse.

115

Removing a relational wall is always worth the time. So be devoted to your spouse. Take on the "Never Give Up" mentality! Make effort to understand your perspective and the perspective of your spouse. Persevere together. Seek wise counsel when you need to, and be patient with your spouse. Removing a wall can be a difficult process. But your marriage is worth it.

How To Resolve Conflict

*"My dear brothers and sisters, take note of this:
Everyone should be quick to listen, slow to speak and
slow to become angry, for man's anger does not bring
about the righteous life that God desires."*
- James 1:19-20

What comes to your mind when you hear the word 'conflict'? What emotion does this word stir up within you? If you're like most people, the thought of conflict doesn't take you to a mental vacation destination, and you probably do not feel warm butterflies in your heart!

Couples often struggle in the area of conflict. Whether you are a newly wed or a veteran in marriage, conflict cannot be escaped. It will happen! Husbands and wives can be cranky, rude and mean toward one another. So it is important to address this topic. How you handle conflict will determine the amount of time your marriage spends in the Insanity Cycle.

We have to learn how to handle conflict God's way. By doing so, we can experience growth in our marriage. This growth can generate positive momentum that can empower husbands and wives to continue living as one flesh.

Husbands and wives seem to approach conflict in one of two ways. You are either a fighter or a thinker. When a conflict arises, a fighter will jump in quickly. A thinker will sit back and analyze the situation. The goal of a fighter is to be the first person to come out swinging and to quickly gain the upper hand. The goal of a thinker is to stay calm and formulate a plan of action. A thinker can take too much time in planning. And a fighter often jumps into conflict too quickly.

Here is another way of explaining things. If conflict were a military battle, fighters would be like the soldiers carrying machine guns. Each individual bullet may not hold great accuracy, but collectively they would do great damage. Thinkers would be more like the sharp shooters. They may not shoot often, but when they do, they aim to kill.

Since thinkers and fighters are so different, they tend to push each other's buttons. A fighter may view a thinker as scared or weak. A thinker can assume that fighters are emotionally unstable. There can be a sense of pride that is carried on both ends. Both fighters and thinkers may reason that their method of handling conflict is superior to the other person's method.

Which kind of person are you? Do you approach conflict as a fighter or a thinker? More than likely, your spouse is the total opposite!

During the second year of marriage, Melissa and I faced our first major conflict. We were experiencing a collision of perspectives and wills. I thought that I was right and Melissa thought that she was right. Both of us were refusing to budge in our point of views. We were stubbornly holding our ground.

As the argument progressed, I began to feel my blood boiling. It was apparent that she was not able to view the situation through my perspective. It felt like we were speaking different languages! I began to cross the line between being angry and going buck-wild postal.

Understand that I had a temper during my teenage years. There were times when I would lose my cool and begin shouting toward my friends and siblings. On occasion, I was known for kicking doors or punching walls. So I didn't want to go there again! As I felt my blood boiling, I knew that I had to get out of the situation, or I was about to say or do something I would later regret. So I did the only logical thing I knew to do at the time. Without saying a word, I turned and walked out the front door of our home.

After slamming the door, I took a three hour long walk. It was great! I had the opportunity to calm down and think through things. As I walked, I had some good prayer time too. God helped me evaluate my heart and highlighted some areas that I needed to apologize for. That walk really helped me clear my head.

As I walked home, I was feeling much better. In my mind, I pictured Melissa sitting at the dining room table with a tissue in hand. I expected her to be calm and ready to have a heart to heart conversation. As I walked through the front door, she would meet me half-way for hugs and kisses. A flood of apologies would immediately follow. Then we would sit down and resolve our conflict in a matter of moments. But when I walked through the door, reality hit me square in the face. I was facing World War Three!

Understand that I am a thinker. So taking that walk really helped me calm down and make a plan. But Melissa is a fighter. When I left the house, I didn't tell her where I was going or what I would be doing. All she knew was that her young husband suddenly walked out on her in the middle of the night. Melissa felt abandoned! As each second passed, she felt like I had turned my back on her. So it took some time to resolve things that evening.

I share this story with you to let you know that I'm human, just like you. Over the years, I've lost my temper, said things I regret and stuck my foot in my mouth. I can be stubborn and cranky. When I don't get my way, I can pout and hold a grudge with the best of them. There are times when I wonder why a woman like Melissa would choose to marry a guy like me. But I'm thankful she did!

God's Word is the GPS that we need, especially in times of conflict. Conflict can stir up fiery emotions and our feelings can be hurt. During conflict, we often see life through the lens of pain and frustration. We need a fresh perspective to shed light on reality. God's Word holds the power to do that. It gives us practical steps that are proven to work. Instead of following our emotions or thoughts, we must cling to God's Word and follow His ways.

So what does God's Word say about conflict? Plenty! James 1:19 says, *"My dear brothers and sisters, take note of this: Everyone should be quick to listen, slow to speak and slow to become angry."* Can you hear the urgency in this verse? James commands us to *"take note"* of his instruction. It's as if he is shouting, *"Ladies and gentlemen, pull out your highlighters. What I'm about to say is good stuff!"*

So get ready to take some notes. Let's break James 1:19 down together. It is packed with helpful truth! Whether you are a thinker or a fighter, this verse can empower you to resolve past, present and future conflicts in your marriage. Instead of running from conflict, God wants your marriage to grow through it. Although conflict is inevitable, it can be beneficial. If you handle conflict God's way, you will find the resolution your marriage desperately needs!

Be quick to listen...

When your mouth is open, your ears tend to be closed. It is common for husbands and wives to become defensive during conflict. We can make great effort to prove our perspectives. By doing so, we close the door to the opportunity that comes from active listening. Instead of listening to understand, we are only listening to formulate our response. When you choose to be quick to listen to your spouse, you will be able to accomplish the following steps:

1. **Try To Understand Perspectives**

As you and your spouse approach conflict, there will be two perspectives. Both of you will have your own way of looking at things. It is important to understand both perspectives! When we don't take the time to understand perspectives, we will make assumptions. And you know what assumptions can do.

It is easy to make assumptions during conflict. We expect our spouse to think and reason like us. In reality, your spouse is not just like you. You are two totally different people. So you will bring two unique perspectives into a conflict. And each must be examined.

When we don't understand perspectives, we can make false accusations. False accusations can be frustrating. If conflict were a fire, false accusations would be the gasoline. Just when you think the fire is settling down...BOOM! False accusations tend to blow things up. Think about how frustrating these statements can be.

So what you are basically saying is....

I never said that!

Yes you did say that!

By being quick to listen, you can avoid those false accusations. You can also seek to understand the perspective of your spouse. You may think you know everything about your spouse and vice versa. But in reality, you do not. So take the time to listen. It will pay off in the end!

2. Identify The Problem

Now that you understand one another's perspectives, you are ready to identify the problem. More than likely, your perspective is a part of the problem! I recommend that you write out the problem. Try to condense it into one sentence. This can help you calm down and take the focus off one another. This is very important. By taking the focus off one another, you can better examine the problem.

As you establish the problem, be sure to keep the focus on the problem. It is easy to shift our focus from the problem to our spouse. Remember that your spouse is not the problem! You are both on the same team here. So you must work together toward a solution. Keep your eyes on the problem!

3. Acknowledge Pain

Our hearts can be most tender with the ones closest to us. Your spouse can hurt you quicker and deeper than anyone else. As we experience a conflict, we can quickly step on one another's toes. In a matter of seconds, hearts can be throbbing with pain.

Acknowledging one another's pain expresses compassion. Isaiah 53:4 says, "*Surely he took up our infirmities and carried our sorrow...*" This verse shows Christ's compassion. Jesus not only recognizes our pain but is willing to help us overcome it. It is important for your spouse to know that you recognize his or her pain.

By recognizing the pain of your spouse, you will be reminded of your compassion for them. And they will feel valued by you! Your spouse's pain is more important than your desire to be right. Acknowledging pain is a powerful expression of love. It will help wives feel cherished and husbands will feel respected.

After you have recognized the pain of your spouse, you can reveal your own pain. Share your pain with your spouse! They need to know about anything that may affect your oneness. By doing so, you will feel a sense of relief. You will also be one step closer to resolving the conflict.

Be slow to speak…

I can't count the number of times I've put my foot in my mouth! When a thought pops into my mind, I think that it needs to be shared in the heat of conflict. In the moment, it seems like a great thought to be shared. Then it backfires and ends up doing more damage than good.

Words are powerful. They can build us up or tear us down. Every word has a purpose. So we must be careful to use our words wisely by recognizing the power they hold. Proverbs 12:18 says, *"Reckless words pierce like a sword...*" Here is an important truth about words. Once they are spoken, you cannot take them back. Sure, you can apologize. But you cannot fully take back what you've said.

James is telling us to zip our lips. In times of conflict, our words must be few. Think before you speak! Do not utter every thought that comes to mind. In James chapter 3, we are given a strong warning. James 3:5 says, *"The tongue is a small part of the body, but it makes great boasts. Consider what a great forest is set on fire by a small spark."* A reckless word holds the power to spark a minor disagreement into a heated argument.

When you are slow to speak, you can stay on the prevent side of things. Guarding your words in a conflict will help you work through problems with much less collateral damage. Conflict doesn't have to involve casualties! As you guard your words, you will be able to accomplish the following steps:

1. Schedule A Time To Talk

Conflict can stir up powerful emotions. You may feel bursts of anger, pain, resentment or confusion. When conflict becomes heated, our emotions can get the best of us. That's when things can get ugly. All it takes is an unloving or disrespectful comment to send us into a whirlwind of a tantrum.

If you sense that your emotions may be getting the best of you, slow down. Do not feel pressured to discuss the problem any further. Tell your spouse that you need to calm down so that you can think clearly. Be sure to communicate this need with your spouse. Tell them that you need a time out and you will discuss things later. Then go and do something that will help you calm down. Take a walk, ride a bike, go work out or read a book. Whatever it takes to calm down, do it. Let your spouse know where you are going and schedule a time to talk later. It can be as simple as saying, ".I need to calm down! I'm going to take a walk. We will solve this problem when I get back."

Communication is important here. By communicating what you are doing, you can prevent your spouse from feeling abandoned. They won't be left trying to figure out where you are going and if you will be back. This will help your spouse calm down instead of sending them into panic mode. You will face smoother waters when you return. I learned this truth the hard way!

2. Evaluate The Problem Biblically

While you are calming down, take advantage of this time apart. Try to connect with Christ and allow Him to evaluate your heart. Psalm 139:23-24 says, *"Search me, O God, and know my heart; test me and know my anxious thoughts. See if there is any offensive way in me."* At this point, you have established the problem that is causing conflict between you and your spouse. Now you must examine your response.

Find out what God's Word has to say about your problem. If you are struggling to find some verses that apply to your situation, seek out someone who can help you. If you seek out someone, do not spill your guts to them! Your goal is to find out what God's Word has to say, not to gain an audience. So keep your request brief. Simply say, "Can you give me Scripture that addresses this area of life?"

After you gain Scripture, you can evaluate your response to the problem. How does God want you to respond? Does your perspective align with God's desires? Have you responded in a way that would please Christ? Spend some time working through these questions.

As you evaluate your response, focus on yourself. Don't get caught up in playing the blame game. It is easy to find fault in your spouse. Perhaps they have not responded in a manner that pleases Christ. They may have said or done something sinful toward you. Neither you nor your spouse is perfect. So focus on yourself first. More than likely, you have plenty of room to grow!

Be slow to become angry...

Anger is a powerful emotion. It can suffocate your ability to think. James 1:20 says, *"For man's anger does not bring about the righteous life that God desires."* This is stating a powerful truth. As Christian husbands and wives, we hold a common goal. Our goal is to please Christ through our lifestyle. If your life were a road trip, you would set your GPS destination to *"the righteous life that God desires."* James is saying that the road paved by your anger will not help you get where you want to go!

I can remember an argument that Melissa and I had during our engagement. We had limited seats for both the wedding and reception. As we made a guest list, it was too big. So we had to make some cuts. During this process, we both became frustrated. We were both emotionally attached to some of the people on our guest list. How could we mark a close friend or family member's name off the list?

This conflict climaxed during one of our date nights. We were going to one of our favorite Italian restaurants.

During our drive, the conversation experienced a stand still. We had both narrowed our guest list to a minimum but still had too many people on the list!

So we became defensive. I tried to convince Melissa why everyone I selected should stay on the list. She tried to convince me, too. After a few minutes, things seemed to settle down. So we went into the restaurant.

As we began to talk, it quickly became clear that our conflict was not over. At this point, I was getting ticked off. My blood was boiling and it was time for this thinker to gain a victory over Melissa. So I opened my mouth and said the first thing that rolled into my mind. "Well, I wish I would have known that you were this kind of person before I proposed!" I foolishly said. Suddenly Melissa's facial expression revealed the damage my words had done. That statement pierced her heart. If looks could kill, Melissa was guilty of murder in that restaurant. And I deserved it. In that moment, my anger did not bring about the righteous life that God desires. I felt like a jerk.

When approaching conflict, it is important to remain in control of your anger. Catch it early on and deal with it! Whatever it takes to calm down, do it. For anger is a powerful emotion. You must master it or it will master you. Here are practical steps to help you be slow to anger.

1. Avoid 'Why' Questions

The purpose for a question is to gain an answer. Since you cannot jump inside the mind of your spouse, you must use each question wisely. Each question must invite your spouse to share their thoughts or feelings with you.

When people hear the word 'why', they can quickly become defensive. That one little word tends to put people on edge. We can feel like we have to defend our thoughts, feelings and perspectives. So avoid asking any question that starts with the word 'why'.

Be creative here. Think of some ways to re-word your questions. Try to replace the word 'why' with 'what', 'how', 'when' or 'who'. If these replacement words do not work, then get even more creative. For example, instead of asking "Why did you do that?" you can ask, "Can you help me understand the reason for doing this?" This may not seem like a big difference to you. The difference will play out in the response of your spouse.

Sometimes it can be difficult to re-word your questions. When you honestly cannot re-word your question, don't ask it! Totally replace the question with a statement. Instead of asking "Why did you do that?" you can say, "Please help me understand your purpose for doing that."

2. Avoid Exaggerated Statements

It is easy to make bold statements during a conflict. Sometimes we can go overboard. Instead of making an accurate statement, we can exaggerate things. Here are two of the most common exaggerated statements:

- *'You always...'*

- *'You never...'*

When we make one of these statements, we are normally scrapping for words. We reach deep down and try to state a truth so boldly that it closes the discussion. But these statements hold the power to ignite things quickly. It can take your spouse from slightly frustrated to ticked off in a matter of seconds.

What is the big deal about these exaggerated statements? You may be thinking, *Seth, I'm just expressing my feelings through those statements. My spouse knows that I don't really mean 'always' or 'never'.* The reason these statements are a big deal is because they are lies. A half truth is a full lie. As Christian husbands and wives, we must walk in truth. 1 John 3:18 says, *"Dear children, let us not love with words or tongue but with actions and in truth."* God expects husbands and wives to walk in truth together. Compromising the truth is never an option for us. It can lead us down a road of lies, deception and broken trust in marriage.

3. Take Responsibility For Yourself

At this point, you should be able to identify some areas that require an apology. If you struggle in doing this, I'm sure your spouse can help you. What have you said that you shouldn't have said? What behavior do you need to take responsibility for?

This is your opportunity to confess your sins. Take responsibility for anything you regret saying or doing during the recent conflict. Whenever you sin against your spouse, you must confess that sin to Christ and your spouse. 1 John 1:9 says, *"If we confess our sins, he is faithful and just and will forgive us our sins."* This verse promises that Jesus stands ready to accept our confession! So we do not need to fear judgment or condemnation from Christ. There does not need to be a fearful hesitation. For He wants to forgive us!

When we confess our sins to Christ, we gain forgiveness. He will remove our guilt and shame. But our confession doesn't stop with Christ. We must also confess our sins to our spouse. James 5:16 says, *"Therefore confess your sins to each other and pray for each other so that you may be healed."* When you confess your sins to Christ, you find forgiveness. When you confess your sins to your spouse, you will find healing.

4. Forgive Your Spouse

We grow up in a culture that doesn't know how to approach forgiveness. When someone says "I'm sorry" for doing or saying something, it can take people off guard. So they quickly respond by saying, "Oh that's ok" or "No problem." These are not the correct responses. If someone's words or behavior has hurt someone, it is not ok! The correct response is "I forgive you."

What is forgiveness? What does it mean to forgive someone for wronging you? When you forgive another person, you are releasing yourself from trying to judge them. In reality, you are not the judge in the first place! So when you forgive someone, you are handing things over to God. For He alone is our righteous Judge. When you say, "I forgive you", you are literally saying, "I will not hold this against you. I'm releasing everything to God. May He be the Judge between us."

Sometimes it can be difficult to extend forgiveness. Perhaps your spouse has said or done something that deeply wounded your heart. Now you find it difficult to forgive. You may be thinking, *My spouse doesn't deserve my forgiveness!'* or *'I'm not going to let them off the hook this easily!* You may even question if the apology is sincere.

Nobody ever said that forgiveness is easy! In fact, forgiveness is often a difficult process. Christ suffered greatly in order to forgive our sins. It brought high levels of stress, pain, blood and sweat. In order to sustain ongoing forgiveness, Christ ultimately gave up His very life. There is nothing easy about forgiveness. It comes with a price.

Forgiveness can be extremely difficult in marriage, especially when your spouse asks forgiveness for a repeated offense. Understand that forgiveness isn't optional for husbands and wives. Colossians 3:13 says, *"Bear with each other and forgive whatever grievances you may have against one another. Forgive as the Lord forgave you."* Nobody deserves forgiveness! That's what makes forgiveness so special. It brings healing and reconciliation back into marriage.

If you are struggling to forgive your spouse, seek help. Do whatever it takes. Your marriage is worth the sacrifice and time! Schedule an appointment with your pastor, a godly friend, a trusted family member or a Christian counselor. For if you hold onto your pain, the anger will lead to resentment. It will destroy your oneness with your spouse. So seek help.

Wrapping Up

Conflict is a natural part of marriage. You cannot escape it, no matter how hard you try. Whether you are a fighter or a thinker, you will have to deal with conflict from time to time. The goal is to handle conflict biblically. This chapter has provided helpful Scripture and biblical steps to help you do that.

Although it will take time, I hope you will master these steps. For by doing so, your marriage will grow through each conflict. You will learn more about Christ, yourself and your spouse. You will also gain a new perspective about conflict. For it doesn't have to be a scary thing. Who knows? You may even come to welcome the opportunities it can bring.

Let's Talk About Sex

"The wife does not have authority over her own body but yields it to her husband. In the same way, the husband does not have authority over his own body but yields it to his wife. Do not deprive each other..."
- 1 Corinthians 7:4-5

The topic of sex is everywhere! Our culture is saturated with it. Television shows, movies, music, billboards, internet, text messaging and the list could go on. Sex is the hottest topic in our society. It seems to be around every corner you turn these days. And the marketing industry is well aware of the truth that "sex sells." No matter how hard you try, it is impossible to escape the topic of sex.

One of the things I've learned, through life experience and teaching couples, is that many Christians are uncomfortable discussing this topic. That is why I like to use the following illustration. If sex were water, men would be Labrador retrievers and women would be camels. Men think about sex often and will jump at the opportunity to experience it. A wife can wake her husband up in the middle of the night and request sex. She will not hear any complaints! Women, on the other hand, can enjoy sex, but they do not crave it nearly as often as men. This illustration seems to help break the ice and get couples to laugh.

One would think that Christians would be excited to talk about one of God's greatest gifts. It amazes me that, to a large degree, Christians have taken an interesting stance on this hot topic. While the world talks about sex, the Church remains silent. Due to this silence, people are left to form their own answers. We are surrounded by secular "experts" who share lies that are cleverly designed as truth. Sadly, people are believing the lies.

What about you? Are you comfortable discussing the topic of sex? Or do you stand on the sidelines in silence? If you're like most Christian husbands and wives, you have one of two stances when it comes to the topic of sex:

1- No comment!!! The topic of sex is dirty and I refuse to talk about it!

2- Hypocrisy. Some Christians openly preach against sexual sin but hold a secret life of immorality. They may be crafty in fooling fellow believers with their front, but the world clearly sees the hidden contradiction.

The secular world views both stances through a negative lens. Our silence and withdrawal can look like a retreat. We often shy away, pulling back into our safety bubbles. It is common for Christians to be looked upon as naïve. Although the first stance is frowned upon, the secular world views hypocrisy as worse. Some Christians preach boldly from their soap box only to dive into a mud pit afterward. Hypocrisy is despised. Nobody likes a liar!

The correct response to the topic of sex has never been silence. For silence allows lies to spread. Silence not only allows lies to spread in the secular world, but even within the Church. You see, I grew up attending church services regularly, and I have wonderful memories of my home church. But their response to the topic of sex was silence. I honestly do not remember one in depth conversation about God's design for sex. The only times I heard the topic of sex addressed was when sexual immorality was preached against. Understand my heart here. I mean no disrespect to my home church or sermons addressing sexual immorality. But they, like many well meaning Christians, were simply uncomfortable with this topic.

In early elementary school, I formed my own beliefs about sex. To me, sex was a dirty sin. It was 100% wrong, 100% of the time. Why did I believe this? First of all, the adult Christians in my life were silent on the topic. Secondly, my best friend was a young pervert! He managed to find XXX magazines that belonged to his dad and freely shared them with me. From time to time, we would look at them. My heart was overcome with guilt after each glance, but I enjoyed looking at the same time. So I had a collision happening in my mind. The world openly talked about sex and seemed to enjoy it while Christians were silent. So in my mind, I thought that sex was evil.

By second grade, I reasoned that sex had no connection with pregnancy. You see, all the adults in my life were Christians. So I thought that only Christians had children. I reasoned that Christian couples would pray for God to provide them children, and then the wife would become pregnant. Although this sounds crazy for adults, it made sense to me as a child, especially when one of the most popular stories I heard was the virgin birth of Christ. Mary experienced a miraculous birth that did not involve sex. And if God provided a child to Mary and Joseph in that manner, then He must still be doing so today.

My bubble of belief was popped when I was in 4th grade. While riding home on the school bus, my best friend started talking about sex. I told him to shut up, explaining that I was trying to be a good boy that day. I didn't want to get caught up in sinful conversations. Then he proclaimed that sex was not a sin. *Blasphemy!* ... I thought to myself. He continued by adding, "Seth, how do you think that you were brought into this world? Your parents had sex!" At that point, I called him a liar and warned him that I was going to beat him down as soon as we got off the bus. He asked me to go home and ask my parents first. If they never had sex together, then I was free to pound his face. It sounded like a great deal to me! So I agreed, and went home.

After going home, I sat down on the living room couch. My Mom was cooking dinner in the kitchen. How would I introduce this evil topic with my Mom? As the gears turned in my mind, I decided to use some humor. Laughter would be a great icebreaker! So I began our conversation with a chuckle. When my Mom asked what I was laughing about, I said, "My best friend is an idiot. He told me that you and Dad had sex to get us kids." My Mom's initial response was silence. To this day, I wish I could have witnessed her facial expression! After a few moments, my Mom's shaky voice broke the silence. "Well, Seth…he's right," my Mom responded. In that moment, my bubble gum theology of sex was popped.

It is important for Christians to openly talk about sex. We should be the experts speaking about this topic! For we know the God who invented it! Christians have the answers to the world's questions. It is time for us to open our mouths and start talking, for this world needs to hear truth. Lies hurt people! So let the healing of hearts begin today. Let's open our mouths and confront the world's lies about sex with the truth. We cannot remain silent anymore.

What The World Is Saying...

What is the world saying about sex? What are the lies that are circulating throughout our culture? From the home computer to the big screen, sex is being broadcasted for people to see. It is easily viewed and freely available. The world is looking and talking. Here are 3 common lies about sex.

1. Sex is a casual event

This lie is ripping the hearts out of people daily. People are being taught that there is nothing sacred about sex. There is nothing special about it. People can have sex without any emotional consequences. Safe sex is the goal! This lie gives people permission to act upon their lustful desires. It makes great effort to remove long term consequences of having sex outside of marriage.

It is rare for a husband and wife to save their virginity for one another. In our fast-paced culture, patience is not a virtue to be desired. Most husbands and wives enter marriage with emotional scars that stem from embracing this lie. They have been viewing sex through a distorted lens. So they may struggle to sustain a great sex life with their spouse. Marriage will not cause this deadly lie to go away.

Those who are sexually active learn that sex is more than a casual event. Sadly, this life lesson can be spiritually, physically and emotionally painful. Proverbs 4:23 says, *"Above all else, guard your heart. For it is the wellspring of life."* Everything we say, feel and do flows from the heart. The heart is the seat of our emotions, the filter for our thoughts and the root of our behavior. It is impossible to remove emotional bonds from the act of sex! No matter how hard you try, you cannot escape this reality. Many husbands and wives share their emotional wounds or sexual diseases instead of true intimacy. Condoms cannot protect the heart. Sex is not a casual toy to be played with. It creates a powerful bond between people.

2. Sex is for everyone

This lie views the wonderful gift of sex as something common. It removes God's design and replaces it as an expected practice. People are being taught that there is nothing sacred about sex. When you develop feelings for someone, you should have sex. By doing so, you will be able to discern if you will be happy with this person forever.

This lie degrades people. Those who try to justify this lie often compare people to cars. *If you're going to commit your life to someone, you better take them for a test drive first. For you need to know if they can sexually please you!* This lie really gets my blood boiling! People are not cars. We are living beings, not machines. We are created in God's image and come fully packaged with free will, thoughts and emotions.

How do you know if you are ready to have sex with someone? Instead of clinging to solid truth, this lie removes reason. People are encouraged to follow their feelings. When you meet the right person, you will feel the right emotion, which will help you discern when you are ready. By removing reason, our feelings become our GPS. This is a dangerous way to live. For our emotions come and go, shifting with life's circumstances. Although they can enhance our experiences, our emotions were never designed to serve as a GPS.

3. Sex is optional for marries couples

When I highlight this lie, husbands express a positive response. It is common for husbands to shout "Amen!" I've even witnessed husbands giving one another fist bumps and high fives! What would cause this overwhelming applause from husbands?

Let's return to my previous illustration for a moment. If sex were water, husbands would be Labrador retrievers and women would be camels. In most marriages, husbands would like more sex! But many struggle to ask for it. Instead of voicing their need, many husbands keep it to themselves. Some husbands may even think their sexual desires are evil. So they don't ask their wives for more sex. Now if you keep a Labrador caged up for an extended period of time, what will he do when he is let out of that cage? You get the picture here. He probably won't practice a lot of patience in the bedroom. Everything will be in hyper mode! Sex will be a heated sprint instead of the marathon that women enjoy.

When husbands hear me teach about this common lie, they are given permission to ask for more sex. They experience a sense of relief. Their ears hear "Your sexual desires are normal!" Their hearts can be liberated.

Wife, this is a good thing! You may be thinking, *Seth I'm still a camel. How can you expect me to play in the water as much as a Labrador?* I don't expect that. That would be a false expectation. So listen to me. When a Labrador is not caged up all the time, he will be calmer around you. Instead of jumping around like a raging ball of energy, he will be more relaxed. And you will enjoy sex even more. In all areas of life, practice leads to progress.

So if sex is not optional for married couples, does this mean that God commands husbands and wives to have sex? Absolutely! Wife, you are camel and your husband is a Labrador. Just because you can walk through the dessert doesn't mean your Labrador can. He needs more water than you do! So give it to him.

Now let me give a challenge to the husbands here. It is important for men to understand the difference between their sexual needs and desires. Husbands, you must draw the line in the sand here. You must clearly identify your sexual needs. You may want to have sex everyday but you may not need to. But if daily sex is an authentic need, you must communicate that with your wife. The goal is to separate your sexual needs from desires and communicate the needs with your wife.

Sometimes I get a blank stare from husbands when I challenge them to define their sexual needs. Most men have never sat down to evaluate this area of life. Husband, if you are struggling to separate your sexual needs from desires, let me give you a good starting point. Whenever you find yourself overly cranky with your wife for no apparent reason, the crankiness could be stemming from an unmet need. So begin your evaluation from there. Let your wife know that you are trying to identify your sexual needs. Most wives will respond with a willingness to help. And that could lead toward some practice time. Husband, that is a great motivation for working to understand your sexual needs!

Now that I've highlighted three common lies about sex, let's replace these lies with truth. For the truth can set us free! It can liberate us from the chains that hold us back from embracing God's gift of sex. It is time for the Church to pave the way for another sexual revolution. Only this time, Christian husbands and wives will lead the charge. And we will proclaim God's design from the roof-tops. Here are 4 truths to embrace:

The Truth About Sex...

1. Sex is God's wedding gift to be enjoyed by husbands and wives

Genesis chapter two records the very first wedding. God created Eve from Adam's rib and brought her to Adam. Verse 24 says, "*For this reason a man will leave his father and mother and be united to his wife, and the two will become one flesh.*" There is a lot of depth within this verse. It is packed with all kinds of truth for husbands and wives! Although the phrase '*the two will become one flesh*' addresses the spiritual, social and emotional union of husband and wife, it is also talking about the sexual union. This verse contains the first reference to sex in God's Word.

Notice who receives the gift of sex within this verse. It was Adam and Eve. Eve is literally called the wife of

Adam in this verse. So God gave the gift of sex to the very first Bride and Groom, to be enjoyed together.

Hebrews 13:4 says, *"Marriage should be honored by all and the marriage bed kept pure."* God provides two commands in this verse. The first command is that marriage should be honored by all. The marriage relationship is to be sacred! Marriage is to be set apart from all other relationships. Husbands, wives, friends and family must recognize the God-ordained bond in marriage.

The second command is for the marriage bed to be kept pure. How do husbands and wives keep the marriage bed pure? For centuries, many Christians have taken the wrong approach. Many Christians have reasoned that the way to obey this verse is to have less sex. Based on the high divorce rate and frequent displays of sexual immorality among Christians, this approach is not working. So how can husbands and wives keep the marriage bed pure? Husbands and wives should have more sex together!

God gave sex as a gift to husbands and wives. The same God who created the heavens and the earth created sex. And He freely gave it to be enjoyed by husbands and wives. Think about this truth for a moment. Imagine that you are attending your best friend's wedding. The ceremony is beautiful and the reception is filled with celebration. Now it is time for the bride and groom to open their gifts. You are excited! For you put a great deal of time in choosing the wedding gift. You have given lots of thought and feeling into selecting this gift.

You wait patiently as they open several gifts before yours. Now it is time for the couple to open your gift. You lean on the edge of your seat as they pick up your gift. After opening it, they hold it in their hands. You are expecting a huge response. For you have made the needed sacrifices to provide this gift. It represents your love and support of their marriage. Perhaps they will jump up and down for joy. Maybe they will run across the room and hug you. Or they may offer a heartfelt glance in your direction. But instead of responding in these ways, they quickly open your gift and then lay it to the side. Your gift brings no excitement or response from them. They do not acknowledge you in any way.

How would you feel? What would you be thinking? More than likely, you would feel hurt. You may even be angry, thinking that your friend is an ungrateful, spoiled brat.

Sex is God's wedding gift to husbands and wives! He has put great thought and design into his gift. The least we can do is enjoy it! How are you receiving God's wedding gift? Are you enjoying His gift or casting it to the side? When is the last time you thanked him for giving you and your spouse the gift of sex? Gifts are given to be enjoyed. God wants husbands and wives to receive His gift of sex and enjoy it. By doing so, we will be able to resist the temptations to fill our sexual appetites outside of marriage. It will also empower us to keep the marriage bed pure and live as one flesh.

2. Sex should be enjoyed by husbands and wives consistently

This truth should come with shouts of joy! And these shouts of joy should come from the lips of both husbands and wives. I remember a powerful moment from teaching this truth. In one particular class session, the husbands were responding with 'Hallelujahs' and 'Amens'. So I began fueling their passion. I replied, "That's right, husbands! Get excited!" After a few moments of celebration, a wife held up her hand. She looked very nervous while doing so. "Seth, can the wives get excited too?" she asked. I responded with a "Yes! Absolutely!" The room was quickly filled with clapping and shouts of joy from the husbands and wives.

Both husbands and wives have sexual needs. God wants those needs to be fulfilled within the marriage relationship. So it is important to communicate your sexual needs with your spouse.

There is a concerning trend in marriages today. Husbands and wives experience high levels of sex during the early season of marriage. Then it tends to fade away. When newly weds proclaim their fun-loving excitement with veterans in marriage, they are met with depressing remarks. *"Enjoy sex while it lasts!" "You are just a newly wed." "Once you settle into marriage, sex will be a thing of the past."* How depressing! It bothers me that

Christians would say things like this. 1 Corinthians 7:4-5 says, *"The wife does not have authority over her own body but yields it to her husband. In the same way, the husband does not have authority over his own body but yields it to his wife. Do not deprive each other except perhaps by mutual consent and for a time, so that you may devote yourselves to prayer. Then come together again so that Satan will not tempt you."*

God gave sex as a gift to husbands and wives. This gift is not to be confined to the newly wed years! Although the frequency of sex may not remain at high levels throughout the years, sex is intended to be enjoyed consistently. It is more than a toy to become bored it. It is a powerful gift that helps husbands and wives experience ongoing oneness

3. **One (Not all) of God's purposes for sex is to have children.**

If you have been living in a childhood bubble similar to mine, I do not apologize for popping it! Babies are not given through storks or prayers alone. Sex is a gift that can give children. Genesis 1:28 says, *"Then God blessed them and said to them, 'Be fruitful and increase in number."* I love this command! God literally commands husbands and wives to have sex together. By doing so we may be blessed with children.

Maybe you are wondering why I'm sharing this truth with adults. If you are a parent, share this truth with you children! Do not allow them to form their own bubble gum theology about sex. You may be thinking, *Seth, my child is too young to discuss the topic of sex.* Remember my previous story. I was a young child when I began thinking about sex. And that was in the 1980's!

The topic of sex is everywhere. As parents, we are the primary spiritual leaders in the lives of our children. They should hear truth from us before they hear the lies of this world. If they hear the lies first, they may struggle to accept the truth. Give your child the truth about sex before they experience an embarrassing moment like I did with my Mom.

4. Sex unlocks the door to intimacy (oneness)

Sex is the gift that keeps on giving! When husbands and wives enjoy God's gift, they will be drawn together as one. Genesis 2:24 says, *"This is why a man leaves his father and mother and is united with his wife, and they shall be one flesh."* Some of the greatest conversations can take place after sex. As a wife cuddles next to her husband, she will notice that he is able to talk more openly about his feelings, intimate thoughts and dreams in life.

God designed sex to open the door to intimacy. Sex and intimacy are intended to go hand in hand, together. They are like cookies and milk. You can't fully enjoy one without the other!

Too many couples do not understand this truth. In fact, husbands and wives tend to define intimacy in different ways. If you ask a husband to define intimacy, he will likely say "Sex!" The wife normally defines intimacy as 'being close'. Husbands can reduce sex to physical pleasure. Instead of drawing close to their wife during sex, they focus on their own physical pleasure in order to have a 'Big O'. Wives thirst for intimacy. Instead of walking through the door that sex provides, they can withhold sex from their husband.

Sex is a powerful force that unites husbands and wives. It unlocks the door to intimacy. Husbands, draw close to your wives during and after sex! Sex is more than physical pleasure. Wives, give it up to your husband! If you want to have those long pillow talks, walk through the door that sex provides.

How does sex unlock the door to intimacy? When a husband and wife enjoy sex as God intended, something beautiful happens in their relationship. Sex is not a tool for gratifying selfish desires. Rather, it is shared to meet one another's need for intimacy.

When a husband and wife have sex for the purpose of meeting one another's needs, they move from "me" to "we". Before marriage, we had the tendency to look out for ourselves. Our mentality was individualistic. Most of our decisions were based on how we, as individuals, could benefit the most. But marriage requires a totally different mentality. Our decisions should be based on the benefit of our marriage relationship. What will be best for my marriage? This question must be our primary method of discernment.

Moving from a "me" to a "we" mentality is a huge shift. It can be extremely difficult. There will be times that we will progress and times when we stumble into old patterns of thinking. God's gift of sex helps husbands and wives start, strengthen and sustain intimacy. It helps the two individuals become one.

I hope this chapter has been helpful for you. If you're like most Christians, sex can be an uncomfortable topic to discuss. But silence is not the right response! God has given sex to husbands and wives to enjoy. We shouldn't be ashamed of it. Start talking about sex with your spouse and teach your children about this wonderful gift in age appropriate ways. Sex is not a dirty secret. It is God's gift for husbands and wives. Our God is pro sex! So I say praise Him! May the 'Amens' and fist bumping begin, for we have reason to celebrate.

Financial Foundations

"My God will meet all your needs according to his glorious riches in Christ Jesus." -Philippians 4:19

I love being a Dad! It is one of life's greatest adventures. The road of fatherhood is paved with laughter, tears, wrestling matches, diapers, tickling, guidance, walks, talks, discipline, stories, play grounds, potty training, songs, prayers, temper tantrums, bath-time jokes and the absence of sleep. There is never a dull moment!

My son, Judah, is about to turn four. If he were in charge of creating the major food groups, we would have one for popsicle. He loves to eat popsicles! But dinner is a different story. Sometimes he doesn't want to eat his dinner. He will take a few bites and then slide out of his chair, disappearing under the table. Suddenly, he will crawl up into my lap. His blue eyes will look at me with a big grin across his face. "Daddy, can I have a popsicle?" he asks.

The next few moments turn into our negotiation time. The outcome depends on Judah's response.

"Judah, you need to take three more bites of your food," Melissa or I will say. Judah's next move is to negotiate by condensing the three bites into two. "Two bites of food for a popsicle?" he asks. Melissa and I will hold to our original expectations of three bites. At this point, Judah will do one of two things. He will either eat his three bites or have an emotional melt-down. Although I prefer the first response, Judah has free will to choose.

When Judah has an emotional meltdown, he becomes extremely stubborn. His mind focuses on his goal of eating a popsicle. That is the only thing that exists in his little world! At this point, negotiation time is over. Melissa and I will respond by pointing him toward his dinner. Now in my mind, it is an easy equation. Judah + 3 Bites of Food = Popsicle. But in Judah's mind, he thinks, Judah's Tantrum = Popsicle.

As I witness the meltdown unfold, it can be frustrating. During the tantrum, Judah seems to lose his ability to reason. He cannot discern the difference between his desire and his need. He thinks that he needs a popsicle because he is hungry. But Melissa and I understand that he needs his dinner for nourishment. The popsicle cannot serve as dinner.

Where do these childish tantrums come from? What would cause a cute child to become a little terror? Tantrums often come from selfish desires. Judah wants a popsicle on his terms. When he doesn't get his way, he throws a temper tantrum. Now before we step up onto our self righteous parenting soap boxes, we need to examine ourselves. For the apple doesn't fall too far from the tree. As husbands and wives, we can throw our own tantrums!

I cannot count the number of times that I've thought *If only I had...*

- *That car!*

- *That house!*

- *That salary!*

- *That lifestyle!*

These are selfish thoughts. They can lead us down a road of heartache. If we allow the thoughts to take root, they will grow into envy and an attitude of entitlement. *I deserve that! If that person can have that, why can't I? It's not fair! I want that!*

An attitude of entitlement blinds us to reality. Our eyes become so focused on what we don't have that we become ungrateful for what we do have. And we can throw our own self- pity-party.

Sometimes it can be difficult to discern our wants from our needs. We may need transportation. But instead of purchasing an affordable used car, we finance the flashy newer model. Or we may need a new phone. Instead of going for the basic model, we reach for the one with the most toys. Sure, it may cost more money, but we need the best! Our hands tend to reach for the shiniest accessories without evaluating the cost. The outcome can be financial stress.

Are you experiencing financial stress? If you are like most husbands and wives, you probably are. Financial stress is considered one of the leading causes of divorce. It is a burden that seems too heavy to carry. The stress can cause husbands and wives to snap at each other. A husband acts unloving toward his wife. The wife can come across as overly critical rather than supportive. I often listen as husbands and wives say, "If we didn't have money problems, our marriage would be healthy!" Although this statement is a common perspective, it is not reality.

Marriage problems actually have little to do with finances. In reality, our finances are connected to our character. Financial problems can reveal our level of spiritual maturity or immaturity. When our bills exceed our budgets, we experience high levels of stress. How we respond to this stress reveals a lot about us. Who do we trust as our provider? How do we handle what has been entrusted to us? How will we respond to unwanted debt? Will we face our obstacles as one flesh? Will we trust God for wisdom and discernment? Or will we turn from His ways?

This chapter brings no judgment or condemnation. Most husbands and wives have experienced the stress of unwanted debt! So no stones will be thrown today. The purpose for this chapter is to give you hope by providing biblical guidance. No matter how high your financial stress may be, God still wants you to be faithful to your spouse. He still expects you to walk together as one flesh.

God's Promise of Provision

God is our Provider! He promises to provide for our needs. Philippians 4:19 says, *"My God will meet all your needs according to his glorious riches in Christ Jesus."* Hear the promise in this verse. God is saying that He will meet *all* of your needs. Will you and your spouse trust Him?

It is important to understand the difference between your wants and needs. A clear perspective of reality will fuel your trust in God. It will also help you recognize His hand at work in your life. Understand that there is nothing wrong with having wants. But when we see our wants as authentic needs, we expect God to provide. When we do not receive what we want, we can throw a tantrum! So recognize the difference between your wants and needs. Remember that God looks at life through the lens of eternity. An authentic need will always hold an eternal value.

As you trust God to provide for your needs, make sure that you do the natural. If we are expecting God to do the supernatural, we must be faithful in the natural. What does this mean? It often means rolling up our sleeves. Be willing to work hard and shed some sweat. When God provides, He normally works through our opportunities. So resist passivity and seize every God-given opportunity.

Building A Solid Foundation

One of the most important steps in building a home is selecting the proper foundation. If the foundation is solid, the home will stand firm, withstanding the test of time. If the foundation is shaky, the home will not last. Jesus spoke about this topic in the book of Matthew. Matthew 7:24-27 says, *"Therefore anyone who hears these words of mine and puts them into practice is like a wise man who built his house on the rock. The rain came down, the streams rose, and the winds blew and beat against that house; yet it did not fall, because it had its foundation on the rock. But everyone who hears these words of mine and does not put them into practice is like a foolish man who built his house on sand. The rain came down, the streams rose and the winds blew and beat against that house, and it fell with a great crash."*

In this story, Jesus talks about two homes. One home was built by a wise man and the second home was built by a foolish man. Both homes had to face difficult seasons of life, as each one experienced great storms. The harsh winds and heavy rains blew and beat against each home. But only one stood firm. What was the difference between the two homes?

The wise man understood the significance of a firm foundation. He built his home upon a foundation that would last. The foolish man simply built his home upon the first convenient plot of land that he could get his hands on. A plot of sand was more convenient than searching for solid ground. It was probably cheaper, too.

What financial principles are you building your marriage upon? Are you patiently following God's design? Or do your hands reach for anything that offers momentary convenience? Building a financial foundation upon God's principles is not the easiest path to take. It requires great sacrifice and determination. But it leads to a solid foundation. And your marriage will be able to weather all of life's storms as one flesh.

No matter what financial season of life you are in, God's principles work. He will bless you for following

His ways. You may not have all of your wants but He will provide for each and every need! Here are 5 biblical principles to build your finances upon:

1. **Walk As One Flesh**

What does it mean to walk as one flesh, financially? It means that you are both on the same page! Although one of you may pay the bills, both of you must create the budget and live by it. You must both take ownership of the budget. Matthew 19:6 says, *"So they are no longer two but one. Therefore what God has joined together, let man not separate."*

I also recommend that you hold joint checking and savings accounts. Now it is ok to have a separate checking account for a business but you must walk as one flesh in your personal finances. God's design for marriage is for husband and wife to walk as one flesh. This means that we work together in all areas of life, including finances.

What about prenuptial agreements? There is never a good reason to have a prenuptial arrangement in your finances. If you do not fully trust the person you are marrying, you need to work on building that trust first. Prenups operate under the terms of a contractual agreement. Marriage is not a contract but a covenant! If you cannot trust your fiancé with your money, why would you trust them with your heart?

What is the difference in a contract and a covenant? A contract is based upon distrust and selfish interests. A covenant is based on trust and selfless motives. Do you see the difference here? Establishing a prenuptial agreement is planning for divorce. You are entering marriage with a planned exit strategy.

Walk together as one in your finances! Although one of you may be more skilled in managing the finances, both of you must be included in some way. So get on the same page and walk hand in hand in your finances.

2. **Bring the Tithe To God**

Notice that I said *bring* not *give* the tithe. Imagine that one of your friends asks to borrow your car. When they are finished with your car, they will return the car to you. They do not give the car to you, for your car already belongs to you. It is your possession! Your friend simply brings it back to you. Do you see the difference? Leviticus 27:30 says, "*A tithe of everything from the land, whether grain from the soil or fruit from the trees, belongs to the LORD.*" A tenth of our income belongs to the LORD, and He commands that we return it to Him.

Now imagine that your friend borrows your car. What would you do if they never returned it? You would be angry! You would demand what is rightfully yours. Your friend would be considered a thief for keeping what does not belong to them. And you probably wouldn't be hanging out in the immediate future. For their theft would affect your relationship.

It is the same way with the tithe. God has blessed us by providing for our needs. And He has given us a pretty sweet deal. He only asks for us to return ten percent of our income to Him. And we get to keep the additional ninety percent! God could have turned it the other way around. He could demand ninety percent and allow us to keep ten percent. But our God is a generous God!

The tithe is a matter of faith. It reminds us who is providing for our needs. God is our Provider! Now I know what some of you may be thinking. *Seth, I provide for my family! I work hard to put food on the table!* Who blessed you with your job? Who blessed you with the ability to work? Who created your mind? Who created your body? You see, God is the source of provision. The tithe helps us recognize His hand at work and be thankful for our blessings.

Proverbs 3:9-10 says, *"Honor the LORD with your wealth, with the firstfruits of all your crops; then your barns will be filled to overflowing, and your vats will brim over with new wine."* These verses are packed with God's promises! If we bring the tithe to God, we are honoring Him with our wealth. And God will bless us for doing so. How will He bless us? He will not only provide for our needs but will do so abundantly. Husbands and wives, this is a promise worth chasing after!

Some of you may be thinking *Seth, you have no idea how tight my budget is. We would love to tithe but we cannot afford it.* Friend, I understand the stress of a tight budget. A tight budget brings lots of temptation. But a tight budget does not give us reason to disobey God. If we are to receive His blessings, then we must obey His commands. Once again, the tithe is a matter of faith. If you can trust your eternal soul to Christ, you can trust Him with your wallet.

Here is one truth I've learned about tithing. When someone says that they cannot afford to tithe, I respond with these questions. How is that working for you? Are you hitting your budget consistently? Are you able to put some money into savings? After working through these questions, the person can see a clear view of reality. Most Christians who do not tithe due to a tight budget are not even able to pay their bills. We cannot afford to withhold the tithe from God! He promises to provide for our needs. So we must trust Him.

When Melissa and I became parents for the first time, we made some major financial shifts. We made these shifts so that Melissa could stay home with Judah during the infant and toddler years. This was very important to us so we have been willing to make sacrifices. There have been some months when we honestly did not know how we would reach our budget! It was very tempting to withhold our tithe. There were countless areas that would benefit from that money. We overcame these temptations, and God has blessed us for it. We may not have all that we want, but God has provided for each and every need.

My family recently vacationed in Tennessee. We were looking forward to spending some quality time with family and friends. As our vacation drew near, I was praying for God's provision. For I didn't know how we would pay for gas! Due to some emergency expenses, gas money for the vacation was not in our budget. So the temptation to withhold the tithe was great. It took a great deal of faith to write that tithe check!

After one of our Sunday church services, a man walked up to me with a smile on his face. I had never met this guy before. He simply said, "Seth, God told me to bless your family with this." He stuck a wad of cash in my hand and told me that he loves me. As the man walked away, I thanked him. God provided the gas money for my vacation through that man's generosity! God not only provided for my needs. He provided abundantly!

3. **Learn To Be Content**

This biblical principle is crucial for us to apply. Whether you are debt free or up to your nostrils in debt, you must learn what it means to be content. The apostle Paul embraced this principle and lived by it. Philippians 4:12-13 says, *"I know what it is to be in need, and I know what it is to have plenty. I have learned the secret of being content in any and every situation, whether well fed or hungry, whether living in plenty or in want. I can do everything through him who gives me strength."*

The above verses proclaim a major victory in Paul's life. He had reached the point in his faith where he was content. He didn't rely upon food, money, possessions or fame to feed his body or soul. Jesus Christ was Paul's source for that. For Paul, his relationship with Christ was enough.

True contentment brings lasting peace. Events and possessions only bring a temporary sense of peace. That is why people are always buying the newest car models and appliance upgrades. We are sold lies that promise peace. For we live in a culture that operates on marketing practices. We are led to believe that we can find contentment through an event or a purchase. If you spend big bucks on a Disney World vacation, your dreams will come true! Or if you purchase a sweet ride, you will be content. Contentment is not found through an event or possessions. It can only be found through Jesus Christ.

Is Jesus Christ enough for you? If your home, your car, your money and possessions were stripped from you, would Jesus be enough? We must chase after the wonderful gift that the apostle Paul found. He learned that Jesus Christ is enough. Through Christ, we can find lasting contentment.

There is power in being content. Contentment affects all areas of life. It opens our eyes to our numerous blessings. Instead of focusing on what we do not have, we will recognize the provision God has already given to us. Contentment can transform a small house or apartment into a home.

4. **Get Out Of Debt**

Proverbs 22:7 says, *"The rich rule over the poor and the borrower is a servant to the lender."* Ouch! Let's be honest here. Nothing good comes from debt! It is easy to get caught up in the buzz that comes from financing something. But the buzz quickly leaves us with a startling reality. We are chained to ongoing payments! Instead of owning our stuff, our stuff seems to own us.

Perhaps you are hoping that I will provide some easy steps toward eliminating your debt. I wish I could do that for you. But getting out of debt is not an easy road. That's why so many husbands and wives continue to be shackled to their debt. The key to overcoming debt rests in your response to it.

Most husbands and wives respond to debt like an ostrich. When the stress of debt comes into sight, we run away. We will stick our head in the first hole that we come to. In our minds, we reason, *If I ignore my debt, it may go away.* While we are hiding, the interest rates continue to grow and the monthly bills never stop reaching our mail box.

Ron and Olivia have been married for three years. Their marriage has become very stressful. One of their biggest stresses comes from the area of finances. They are desperately seeking ways to get out of debt. It seems like their monthly living expenses never meet the budget. Olivia blames Ron and he blames her. Deep inside, they both feel guilty for this terrible season of life.

Where did their financial stress come from? It began during their dating years. When Ron knew Olivia was the right girl, he went shopping for an engagement ring.

Since he wanted the best for Olivia, he wanted to purchase a large diamond. Ron didn't want a lack of cash flow to stand in the way of sweeping Olivia off her feet. So he found a desirable ring and financed it. It didn't seem like a big deal at the time. And Olivia was so happy with the size of her diamond!

As Ron and Olivia planned their wedding, they wanted a big day. Both of them had friends and family who would like to attend the ceremony. Neither of their home church buildings were large enough for all of their guests, so they decided to rent a beautiful resort for the weekend. Ron simply placed the fees on one of his credit cards. It didn't seem like a big deal at the time.

As they discussed honeymoon options, they decided to go on a cruise to the Bahamas. They found a great deal with a local travel agency. Although they paid for the deposit up front, the rest of the honeymoon was put on Olivia's credit card.

After the honeymoon, they decided to purchase new furniture for their apartment. After visiting several stores, they found the perfect living room sofa with matching tables and chairs. And this particular store offered zero interest for the first year! Ron and Olivia reasoned that they would aggressively pay things off before the interest would kick in. So they got a new credit card from the furniture store and placed their furniture purchase on it.

After six months of being married, the bills were beginning to take their toll. Ron and Olivia became stressed with their financial commitments. They knew that they needed to make a plan to get out of debt soon. Their intentions were interrupted by the death of Ron's car. So they went car shopping. They were able to make a down payment to get a good interest rate. But they had to get another loan to cover most of the purchase.

The next couple of years were scary for Ron and Olivia. They lived as typical ostriches. Although they understood they were in debt, neither of them wanted to evaluate the damage. So they tried to get by from month to month. When needed, they would skip a monthly payment here and there. This, in turn, would cause the interest rates to go up.

Now Ron and Olivia are constantly worried about their debt. It has robbed their intimacy and haunts their marriage. What happened to the joy they once shared?

Ron has buried himself in eighty hour work weeks in order to hide from reality. Olivia works two jobs and tries to pick up extra hours when the opportunity arises. Their stress is bottled up inside, leaking out with the occasional argument. Both of them feel like their marriage has become a cage.

Can you identify with Ron and Olivia? Is debt a major stress in the life of your marriage? It is time for you to get a handle on things. Stop hiding like an ostrich and take your stand. Don't let your stress separate your oneness in marriage!

The best way to get out of debt is to follow these two steps. The first step is to face your debt. Examine the damage and understand it. Before you can overcome any obstacle, you have to evaluate it. So collect those bills and lay them all out. Know how much you owe and to whom you owe the money..

The second step is to make a plan with your spouse. Seek wise financial counsel! Although it may cost you some time and resources, it is worth the investment. It may take months or years to get out of debt. But every journey begins with the first step. Map out your plan with your spouse. And walk it out together!

5. Grow As A Giver

This principle is perhaps the most difficult. Our God is the most generous Giver. And He expects us to follow His example. What makes this principle so difficult? Let me give you an example.

Imagine that you are driving home from work. It has been a long day and you've put in some long hours. Now you are looking forward to a relaxing evening at home. As you approach an intersection, you notice a guy on the side of the road. His clothes are dirty and his hair is unkempt. He is holding a sign that says, *"I'm hungry."* What is the first thought that comes to your mind?

I confess that I sometimes struggle in situations like these. When I see someone like this guy, I tend to think *I've worked hard for my money! This guy is simply standing on the side of the road. Why should he gain from my labor? Besides, he is probably hungry because he is too lazy to work.* Although I may give to the man, these thoughts often run through my mind. And I'm not proud of them either.

I recently came across a troubling passage of Scripture. It has been convicting my heart and challenging me to grow as a giver. Luke 6:30-35 says, *"Give to everyone who asks you, and if anyone takes what belongs to you, do not demand it back. Do to others as you would have them do to you. If you love those who love you, what credit is that to you? Even sinners love those who love them. And if you do good to those who are good to you, what credit is that to you? Even sinners do that. And if you lend to those from whom you expect repayment, what credit is that to you? Even*

sinners lend to sinners, expecting to be repaid in full.
But love your enemies, do good to them, and lend to them
without expecting to get anything back. Then your
reward will be great and you will be sons of the Most
High..." This passage commands us to give to everyone
who asks. There doesn't seem to be any crafty loop holes
within these verses.

God is the most generous of givers! He provides for
our needs and blesses us beyond our expectations. He
wants us to grow in His likeness. He expects us to
approach those in need with a generous spirit. Who are
we to judge others? That is not our place in this world.
God is the One who can see the motives of the heart. So
instead of placing a label on someone in need, we must
follow God's command to give.

Melissa and I were recently teaching this principle to
a large group of couples. A wife expressed a valid
concern. "Shouldn't we be wise with our money? If
someone uses our money to feed an addiction, are we
enabling them?" she asked. So I asked the couples to
openly share their opinions. It turned into a lively
discussion.

During the discussion, someone shared a great idea.
This person traveled daily through a particular region of
their city that had several homeless people in need who
often asked for food at intersections. This person wanted

to be wise and avoid stepping into the role of an enabler. So they prepared small bags of food and toiletries and freely shared these with those in need. What a great idea! She was being wise and obedient.

God wants us to be wise with our money. He also wants us to give to those in need. Neither of these expectations cancels the other. The two go hand in hand. So we must grow in wisdom and our ability to give. This will empower us to truly love others and meet authentic needs.

Final Financial Thought

I wish I could say that I'm where I want to be financially. But I'm not. Like you, my life still has plenty of room to grow. But Melissa and I are growing together. We know what it's like to live on a tight budget. We understand the temptation to withhold God's tithe to get ahead. But we also know the taste of victory that comes through obedience. We can honestly proclaim that God has met all of our needs, and He continues to do so! God always blesses our obedience.

I want to remind you that there is no judgment or condemnation in this chapter. Remember that James 3:2 says, *"We all stumble in many ways."* We have all fallen short in the area of finances! So no matter what financial season of life you are facing, I want to encourage you.

Do not point a blaming finger toward your spouse. Reach out and take hold of their hand. Confess what needs to be confessed, and offer forgiveness to one another. Start walking together as one flesh in your finances. Do not allow financial stress to separate your oneness. By facing your obstacles together, your oneness will be strengthened. And our God will sustain you.

Use God's principles as your financial foundation. He loves you and will provide for your needs. Remember that authentic needs hold eternal value. Overcome temptations that lead to financial disobedience. God loves you dearly, and He will never let you down. Seek Him, trust Him and obey His financial principles. Then you will be on the road that leads to contentment.

Be Devoted

*"They devoted themselves to the apostles' teaching and
to the fellowship, to the breaking of bread and to prayer."*
- Acts 2:42

I recently met a good friend for breakfast. We talked
about life, ministry and marriage. Since my friend shares
my passion for equipping husbands and wives to
experience God's best, our voices grew louder as we
brainstormed ways to minister to couples. We didn't
realize how much our voices were carrying!

As we talked, an elderly couple overheard our
conversation. They were sitting in the booth next to us.
The wife gave us a compliment. "We love to see young
people walking with the Lord," she said. Once the ice
was broken, her husband began talking to us, too.

The typical questions began to be exchanged. *What
is your name? What do you do for a living? Where do
you go to church? Where are you from?* The couple
shared how they were originally from east Tennessee.
They were actually from a small town close to my
hometown! So we were able to find some common

ground quickly. It is always neat to meet other people who are familiar with your hometown, especially when you are from a very small one!

One of the characteristics that stood out in this couple was their great sense of humor. The longer we talked, the more it came out. The husband began to share some jokes. "My wife is an angel. She is always flying around, harping about something!" he said. Then he would chuckle while everyone laughed. "You know, boys, my wife worships me. She gives me three burnt offerings a day," he continued. That guy missed his calling as a stand-up comedian!

His wife was funny, too. She would immediately have a witty remark to bounce back. She was always two steps ahead of him. My friend and I enjoyed their company. That couple was the life of our breakfast party!

My friend asked the couple how long they had been married. We learned that they were married over 60 years ago. We were both amazed. This is rare to witness in today's times. But something else caught my attention. They were still enjoying one another's company! They weren't referring to marriage as a 'ball in chain' or in any other negative way. This couple didn't criticize our amazement either. They took joy in the fact that they were still married. I could tell that they had a

One Flesh marriage. This husband cherished his bride, and she respected him. They were a walking testimony that marriage can last!

As the couple left, my friend and I watched them walking in the parking lot. We started laughing when we noticed what they were driving. A Jeep Wrangler! How many elderly couples have you seen driving a Jeep Wrangler? It seemed to fit their young hearts.

We also noticed the husband open the door for his bride. It was moving to witness him treat her like his queen. Throughout their many years together, he was still her gentleman. After opening her door, the husband walked around to his side and slowly climbed in.

As we watched the couple drive away, we began to discuss the blessing we had received from spending time with them. It was as if their joy and determination rubbed off on us. In a world packed with relational confusion and deception, it was refreshing to see the simplicity of God's design for marriage. We were reminded that God's ways still work. And there are real life couples who are experiencing God's best!

I'm thankful that I was able to meet that couple. They were an inspiration to me. In a world where marriages and families are falling apart, it is reassuring to see husbands and wives sustain oneness in marriage. I'm sure that elderly couple has faced some major obstacles over the years. But the obstacles didn't separate their oneness. After 60 years, they remained faithful to one another. I hope that God blesses them with many more years together!

If God grants me the blessing of a long life, I want to spend my years with Melissa. As we face obstacles that threaten our oneness, we will overcome them together. I will cherish her until the day I die. And I am confident that she will respect me until the day she breathes her last breath. When our hair turns white, we will still be holding hands. When all is said and done, I want our marriage to stand firm through the test of time.

What about you? Do you want the same for your marriage? Do you want to be faithful to your spouse? Do you want to experience God's best? Do you want to overcome life's obstacles with your spouse? I think you do! You probably would have thrown this book aside if you didn't want a lasting marriage.

What is the secret to a lasting marriage? How can husbands and wives be confident that their vow will endure the test of time? What can you do to insure your marriage?

We live in a culture that despises God's design for life. We are taught to look after number one at all cost.

Selfish desires are fueled with a sense of entitlement. *What's in it for me? How can I benefit from this? My needs are not being met so I will go elsewhere. I deserve better!* Divorce has become a socially acceptable option for husbands and wives. When the going gets tough, many husbands and wives choose to get out.

If you want to insure that your marriage will last, you must choose to be devoted to your spouse for life. You must choose to walk through the good times and the bad. Your expression of love and respect cannot be dictated by life's circumstances. You must fulfill your God-given role at all cost. Husband, you must cherish your wife, even when she is disrespectful. Wife, you must respect your husband, even when he is unloving toward you. Nothing can be allowed to separate your devotion to one another.

Marriage is not easy. It is a holy relationship designed by God Himself. You cannot live out God's design without Him. Husbands, you must be empowered by Christ daily to be the husband He has called you to be. Wives, you must be empowered by Christ to be the wife He has called you to be. It is impossible to experience God's best without Him! You must both walk with Christ, together.

I know what some of you may be thinking. *Seth, how can you make a statement like that? I know several couples who have been married for years and they are not Christians! And marriage seems to be working for them.* It is possible for husbands and wives to stay together without Christ. But we cannot experience Christ's best without a relationship with Him. If you examine any marriage that lacks Christ, you will find that the husband and wife are not truly satisfied.

As I was eating lunch today, a man walked up to me. He asked me how the Journey Church is doing. So I told him about the ways that Christ is transforming lives. This is an exciting season for the Journey! We are in the process of building a new campus so that we can share the Good News with more people and disciple them in Christ's ways. As we talked, he decided to join me for lunch so that we could continue our conversation.

On the surface level, this guy seemed to be doing ok. He told me how he often passes the Journey Church's new property on his drive to work and has been wondering when the new construction would be finished. I gave him a timeframe of when we hope to be moving into our new campus.

He also shared about the blessing of his jobs. In today's economy, this man expressed gratitude for his income. God had blessed him with full-time employment and a part-time job. He was especially passionate about his part-time job of photography. Our conversation went down a road of technical camera terminology that was foreign to me. So I just smiled and nodded.

After a few minutes, the topic of marriage came up. The man told me that he had been married for several years and is faithful to his wife. He went on to share some of his philosophy on marriage. As I listened, he would talk more. As he continued to talk, he became more comfortable in sharing more personal details.

He eventually revealed why he had approached me. "Seth, I haven't told many people this but I feel like I need to tell you," he said. He began to describe what his marriage is really like. For the past five years, this man has been sleeping on the couch. He explained that he and his wife have simply grown apart over the years. She has her life and he has his. He still trusts that she is being faithful to him and claims that he is being faithful to her. They just aren't as close as they used to be. Although he refuses to get a divorce, he isn't really doing anything to strengthen his marriage relationship.

Too many husbands and wives are surviving rather than thriving. The purpose for marriage is more than simply living together. God wants husbands and wives to be more than roommates! He wants us to walk in absolute devotion to Him and one another. How do we live out our devotion to Christ within marriage? What are some things we can do to move from surviving to thriving? How can you ensure that, if you are still breathing, you will be walking with your spouse, hand in hand, after 60 years of marriage?

Our answer rests in God's Word. Acts 2:42 says, *"They were devoted to the apostles' teaching and to the fellowship, to the breaking of bread and to prayer."* A key word in this verse is 'devoted'. The early Christians were devoted to Christ and one another. What does it mean to be devoted? This word means to continue steadfastly. What a powerful concept! It expresses a never-give-up attitude. You celebrate the good and endure the seasons of difficulty. When the going gets tough, you roll up your sleeves and press on.

Devotion is rarely expressed within our society. For we live in a world that searches for loopholes within our commitments. We will sign a paper or give our word in order to gain something we desire. We rush into relationships and purchases without taking the time to count the cost. When the time comes to make needed sacrifices, we hit the road. While we are leaving, we try to convince ourselves that it is not our fault. We can go to great lengths in order to justify quitting.

Marriage requires a high level of devotion. Both the husband and wife must be devoted for life. If you are devoted to your spouse, you will continue to live in oneness with them regardless of life's circumstances.

Being devoted is not a temporary thing. It is an ongoing commitment that is never broken. You are either all in or all out. There is no room for middle ground. One Flesh marriages are not established by chance. They require absolute devotion.

I recently met a couple for biblical marriage counsel. Within the first two minutes, I could tell that they were in crisis. Their body language, voice tones and words expressed anger, resentment and pain. This marriage was on the rocks.

One of my goals in the first session is to let them vent. As they vented, I was able to see their perspectives and emotions. This couple argued and bickered for about fifteen minutes. I was able to pick up on a major area of division within their marriage.

They were living in separate homes. Through a series of questions, I learned that there was no abuse or threat of abuse. This husband and wife had simply chosen to live separately while working out their problems. They allowed their differences to place a physical wedge in their relationship. They lacked oneness.

My next move was to establish their expectations for meeting with me. "What do you hope to gain from meeting with me?" I asked. They both expressed a desire to reconcile their differences so they could experience a healthy marriage. I affirmed their desire for reconciliation and told them that I would gladly teach them God's design for husbands and wives.

My next question was more challenging. "What are you willing to do?" I asked. Both of them assured me that they would make whatever sacrifice necessary to gain a healthy marriage. Their words expressed a determined work ethic. Then I made a quick shift, going back to their living conditions. I needed to see if their words and actions were lining up.

I told them that their living conditions would need to change if they wanted a healthy marriage. If they were willing to roll up their sleeves and work through differences, they needed to be living together. They could not apply the biblical tools to their relationship if they were not living together. This was a great challenge to them, especially for the wife. As a part of their first homework assignment, they were to make a plan to move in together. The plan had to be on a calendar with specific action steps before our next appointment. Although the move didn't have to take place within the week, it had to be in the near future.

Some of you may be thinking that I shouldn't have challenged them in this way. *Come on, Seth! Maybe they need time to work through some things before living*

together again. Where is your sense of patience?
Understand that I am very cautious in these situations. If
there was any hint of abuse, I would have advised
differently. Husbands and wives must be devoted to their
marriage. Devotion means that both feet are in. You
cannot have one foot in and one foot out. Devotion
demands all or nothing. For better or worse, husbands
and wives must stick together.

4 Devotions To Share As Husband and Wife

Now that we've established the importance of
devotion, let's go back to Acts 2:42. This verse says,
*"They devoted themselves to the apostles' teaching and
to the fellowship, to the breaking of bread and to prayer."*
This verse describes the four shared devotions of the
early Church. These devotions served as their method for
expressing their love for Christ and one another, both
corporately and in each individual home. Although Luke
(the inspired author of Acts) was not specifically
addressing marriage in this verse, I think he would agree
with my extended application of the four devotions.

I want to challenge you to live out these devotions
with your spouse. Choose to incorporate them into the
life of your marriage daily. Do not merely read over
them and agree. Apply them!

Remember that the goal is progress. Create an intentional plan for growth. If you already share some of these devotions, plan to practice them more. If any of these devotions are absent from your marriage, start small. Choose one or two days per week to practice the devotions. Be patient! Practice makes progress. Practice them consistently, holding one another accountable. Understand that you will never reach perfection. Practice will not empower you to be perfect but it will help you grow. And that should be our goal!

Before I highlight the four devotions, let me remind you of an important truth. God's design works! It always has and it always will. When couples come to me for marriage counsel, I ask them if they share any of these devotions. Here is an interesting truth that I've found. The couples that come to me for crisis counsel are never practicing these devotions! Let me say this one more time. The couples who come to me for crisis counsel are *NEVER* practicing the following devotions.

Practicing these devotions may not eliminate all of your problems but they will empower you to face them. And you won't be facing the problems by yourself. Christ and your spouse will be right there with you. The following devotions will help you follow Christ with your spouse. I'm confident that your marriage will benefit from applying them.

1. Be devoted to God's Word

God's Word is our authority. It provides guidance for all areas of life. Both husbands and wives must be devoted to God's Word. Psalm 119:105 says, *"Your word is a lamp to my feet and a light for my path."* By following the guidance of God's Word, you will be traveling in the same direction with your spouse. Traveling in the right direction is crucial! Our direction will determine our destination.

Let's say that you want to go on a vacation. You need some rest and relaxation. Your spouse suggests a trip to the beach. Great idea! After identifying which beach you wish to visit, you begin to pack for the trip. You enjoy long discussions about the ocean breeze, waves and the feeling of sand between your toes. Your excitement grows with each passing minute.

As you get in the car, you begin your journey. After forty-five minutes, you notice the GPS isn't working. Since you both are excited about the vacation, you don't want to return home for the other GPS. Although neither of you have been to this specific beach, you are both confident that you can figure things out. *How hard can it be to find the beach?*

After several hours, you are in unchartered territory. You have absolutely no idea where you are. Your eyes begin to read every exit, wondering which one you should take. One exit seems appealing to you while another one appeals to your spouse. Which exit is the right one?

You are confident that your desired exit is the right one. So you begin to explain why your exit of choice makes practical sense. Your spouse disagrees, claiming their preferred exit is the more logical path. In reality, you both could be wrong, but you both are clueless! It is your word against the word of your spouse. As the disagreement progresses, it becomes a battle of who is right instead of a search for how to get to the beach. You need a GPS!

God's Word is our GPS on life. He created us and has a purpose for our lives! When a husband and wife follow the instruction of God's Word, they will walk in unity with Christ and one another. And they will be growing in the right direction. They can be assured that the direction leads them down the road toward a One Flesh marriage. Instead of arguing who is right or wrong, they will submit to the authority of God's Word and reach their desired destination.

Let me address some common questions. Should you read God's Word with your spouse? Or should you read God's Word separately? For some couples, reading at the same time works great. Other couples confess that it feels awkward. My advice is to try both. And make effort to be reading the same section of Scripture that your spouse reads on a particular day. You may enjoy reading at the same time. Or you may find that you enjoy reading separately, coming together later for discussion. The key is to share your devotion to God's Word with your spouse. Avoid the unneeded stress of comparing your method with other couples.

If reading God's Word is new to you, be sure to choose a translation of Scripture that you understand. There are several modern translations you can choose from. Understanding what you read is important! By understanding God's Word, you can seek ways to apply it to your life. Once you have a translation that you can understand, follow these helpful steps:

• *Set a time to read daily.* Think through your daily schedule and choose a specific time that works well for your schedule. Get it on the calendar! I recommend choosing the same time each day, if possible. This will keep things simple and be easier to remember.

I often hear a list of excuses from couples concerning their devotion to God's Word. The most common excuse is a lack of time. *I don't have any free time! My schedule is already over-booked.* If you struggle to set a daily time for reading God's Word, try this. Get up fifteen minutes earlier each day. By doing so, you can create the time without altering your other daily events. Although you may be losing some sleep, you will be adding God's Word to your life. And that is a great exchange! People will find a way to do what is important to them. If you and your spouse are devoted to the authority of God's Word, you must make the time for it.

- *Be realistic.* As you begin reading God's Word daily, remember to keep it simple. Consistency is important. Don't try to read for thirty or forty minutes at a time. Many Christians set unrealistic goals and expect to be Bible scholars overnight. When they don't reach this goal, they feel like failures. You can avoid this let down by setting a realistic goal. Start by reading ten to fifteen minutes a day. And if you hate to read, start by reading five minutes a day! You will grow over time. Start small and add more time as you go.

- *Guard your daily time in God's Word.* Do not give up your Bible reading time for outside activities. By guarding your time, you will be expressing your devotion to God's Word. Except for emergencies, other activities can wait! Do not be afraid to say no to other things. We must keep the main thing the main thing.

2. Be devoted to fellowship.

Fellowship prevents Christianity from becoming stale and keeps things relational. Our faith is more than punching a spiritual time clock. This leads me to an important question. What is the difference in fellowship and friendship? Fellowship is a mutual sharing of faith. Both friendship and fellowship can lead to a relational connection. But only fellowship involves our faith in Jesus Christ. In Matthew 18:20, Jesus said, *"For where two or three come together in my name, there am I with them."* Only Christians can experience the mutual sharing of faith.

Sadly, many Christians do not see the importance of fellowship. Instead of enjoying the mutual sharing of faith, they try to do life alone. Have you ever heard someone say, "I have a personal relationship with Jesus Christ."? When people make this statement, they often mean something else. The word 'personal' often means 'private.' So they really mean, "I have a private relationship with Jesus Christ."

It is important for husbands and wives to enjoy fellowship with one another! We must mutually share our relationship with Jesus Christ. This means that you will be aware of the ways Christ is moving in the life of your spouse, and vice versa. Our faith was never meant to be hidden from others. Matthew 5:14 says, *"You are*

the light of the world. A city on a hill cannot be hidden."
Husbands and wives must follow Jesus Christ together.

It is also important for husbands and wives to be connected to a local church. The Church is the hope of the world! We are the family of God. In order for a family to be healthy, each member must contribute in positive ways. Hebrews 10:25 says, *"Let us not give up meeting together, as some are in the habit of doing, but let us encourage one another."* Life is not always easy. As Christians, we will face many difficult seasons of life. The Church is our extended family. And family must stick together.

Husbands and wives experience multiple blessings through fellowship. Our faith was never intended to be lived out alone. Fellowship opens the door to relational growth with Jesus Christ, our spouse and the Church. Fellowship provides husbands and wives with:

- *Strength* to endure hardships. *"Carry each others burdens, and in this way you will fulfill the law of Christ."* -Galatians 6:2

- *Wisdom* for making difficult decisions. *"He who walks with the wise grows wise."* - Proverbs 13:20

- *Accountability* for overcoming life's temptations. *"Brother, if someone is caught in a sin, you who are spiritual should restore him gently."* -Galatians 6:1

- A *family* to grow with. *"Be devoted to one another in brotherly love. Honor one another above yourselves."* -Romans 12:10

3. Be devoted to breaking bread.

We live in a fast-paced society! We rush here and there, trying to accomplish each of the items on our long to-do-list. At the end of the day, we can sit back and think, *Where did the day go?*

It is easy to lose connection with your spouse in a busy schedule! If you are like most couples, your schedule separates you from your spouse on most days. You spend long hours at work or running errands, only to find yourself exhausted at the end of the day. It is important to find time to reconnect with your spouse.

We all want quality time in marriage. Our hearts crave opportunities for creating lasting memories together. Lasting memories strengthen our oneness and remind us of our special bond. We all enjoy those 'Remember the time...' moments!

Quality time comes from quantity time. Many husbands and wives think they can by-pass quantity time and still create quality time together. This is impossible! If your marriage is going to experience quality time, you must create time to be with your spouse. One of the easiest ways to do this is to share a meal together.

Think back to the dating days. What activities did you enjoy while dating your spouse? More than likely, your dates included a meal of some kind. And you enjoyed those dates! By sharing meals together, you were able to talk about life, your dreams and the obstacles you want to overcome. Something almost magical happens when we share a conversation over a meal. A common meal becomes an opportunity for our hearts to connect.

Start carving out some quantity time by sharing meals with your spouse. Sit down and enjoy some good food. Laugh together. Tell your spouse about the day's events. You'll be glad that you did. For you will be creating some lasting memories together.

4. Be devoted to prayer.

Prayer is our life-line to God. It is an open door that never closes, no matter the time of day or night. Prayer allows us to talk to God, sharing our gratitude, questions and frustrations with the One who loves us most. When we pray, our intimacy with God will grow.

Remember the common phrase I highlighted a few paragraphs ago? *'I have a personal relationship with Jesus Christ.'* When Christians use this phrase, they really mean *"My faith is private and is not open to be shared. Back off!"*

Many husbands and wives carry this attitude in their prayer life. They may pray often but do so separately. They rarely pray together. Do you pray with your spouse? It is important for husbands and wives to pray *for* and *with* one another. Many husbands and wives say they pray for each other, but few seem to pray with one another.

What is your spouse praying for? How do you need to be praying for your spouse? These questions can be best answered by praying together. When you pray with your spouse, you will be able to hear their conversation with God. You can have a front-row seat for hearing their prayers. By hearing the prayers of your spouse, you can learn how to pray for them. For prayer reveals our deepest needs.

If you are feeling guilty for not praying with your spouse, that is not my intent. There is no judgement or condemnation here. My desire is to help you experience

God's best for your marriage. In order to experience His best, you must be devoted to prayer.

One of the things I have learned through ministering to couples is that husbands and wives want to pray together, but something seems to be holding them back. Maybe one spouse senses the other is more spiritually mature. They may feel intimidated. Or perhaps a spouse has never prayed out loud. They may be used to praying silently.

Sometimes couples confess that they have tried praying together and it felt awkward. So they stopped. If this describes you, let me offer a word of encouragement. Most new practices feel awkward at first. Think about the first time you rode a bicycle. Were you able to stay up the whole time? Even if you had training wheels, you had to practice. The more we practice something, the more comfortable we will become.

If praying with your spouse is something new for you, be patient. Avoid too much structure. Too much structure may cause prayer to seem forced. Prayer is simply a conversation with God, nothing more and nothing less. You do not have to write down 25 requests beforehand. Simply pray. Share whatever is on your mind with God. Start talking to God with your spouse. By doing so, your intimacy will grow, both with Christ and one another.

Make A Plan

As I type these words, I'm looking at my car insurance bill. The bill is on the counter next to me. It includes the multiple ways that Melissa and I will be covered if we have an accident. As I pick it up, I read over it. It brings a sense of comfort knowing that my family is insured against unforeseen accidents!

In order to receive the insurance coverage, I must pay the renewal bill. No matter how much I agree with the plan, I must do something in order to receive it. My desire for insurance isn't enough. Unless my desire is backed by action, it is useless.

This chapter highlights the four devotions that will help insure your marriage. The power does not rest in the devotions themselves. The power is found in Jesus Christ. And each devotion will help you and your spouse connect with Him.

Do you want to ensure that your marriage is healthy? Would you like for your marriage to weather the storms of life? When all is said and done, do you want to be holding the hand of your spouse, looking back on your years together with joy? If you answer yes to these questions, it is time to prove your answer. It is time to put the four devotions into practice.

Plan a time to discuss these devotions with your spouse. Which one(s) are you currently practicing together? Which one(s) are lacking in your marriage? Make an intentional plan to begin practicing each one. This will provide opportunities to grow together.

It's Never Too Late

*"If my people, who are called by my name, will humble
themselves and pray and seek my face and turn from their
wicked ways, then I will hear from heaven and will
forgive their sin and will heal their land."*
- 2 Chronicles 7:14

From time to time, I will come across some couples
who are skeptical toward God's design for marriage.
When they hear me teach, they wonder if this One Flesh
concept actually works. *Come on, Seth, you mean to tell
me that these ancient principles are still relevant for
marriages today?* I admit that God's design goes against
today's culture. But it works!

Most people believe that upgrades are better than
older models. Why? We tend to reason that newer is
better! That is why people will go in debt for new cars,
new homes, new furniture, new carpet, new clothes, new
appliances, new computers or gadgets. We want
everything new!

I know that times are changing. This world is not the
same as it was in ancient times. We have progressed in

many ways. Although we have experienced significant changes over time, there are certain pillars of society that should never change. Marriage is one of them. God's design cannot be manipulated. It cannot be altered to meet our standards. Why? God's design is already perfect! Why would we want to take on new practices when the older ones have proven true? Instead of searching for the newest marriage fad, we need to cling to something that works. God's design works! We must return to it.

Some skeptics question God's design because of pain and frustration. Although they admit that their current marriage is unhealthy, they hesitate to accept anything else. They have strayed so far from God's design that they question if it is still for them. They think that they've reached the point of no return. Although they may agree that God's design can work for others, they do not think it is available to them.

Perhaps you are carrying some skepticism. Maybe you are facing some major obstacles that hinder your marriage relationship. Or you may have simply lost that special closeness you once shared with your spouse. As you read through this book, your eyes may recognize the fact that your marriage is far from what you'd like it to be. Although you believe that God's design may work for other marriages, you may question if it would benefit yours.

If this describes you, I want to share something with you. You are the reason I am writing this chapter! God's design for marriage is within your reach. It is not too late for your marriage. God's design is not only for those '*other*' couples. It was created for you, too! How do I know this to be true? My eyes have witnessed the restoring power of Jesus Christ time and time again. No matter what you've said or what you've done, you can experience a one flesh marriage! My God is bigger than your worst case scenario. And He holds victory in store for those who trust in Him. You are just one prayer away from change.

A Restoration Story

If there is a rock bottom in marriage, David and Olivia were there. Over the past several years, they had been living under extreme financial stress. Due to the economy, they lost two homes and were barely living from pay check to pay check. Each day was filled with calls from creditors they couldn't pay. Their stress caused them to express unloving and disrespectful behavior toward one another. Just when they thought things couldn't get worse, Olivia found out that David was having an affair. This is when they came running for help.

Olivia felt like her world was caving in on her. Her heart was raw with the pain of betrayal. Would she choose to walk through the restoration process with David? Or would she choose to walk away?

Her emotions were like a roller coaster. One moment she felt like holding David in her arms and weeping. The next moment she would feel like punching him in the face. She struggled with the decision that was before her eyes.

David was broken. He couldn't believe that he hurt the one he loved most. "How could I do such a thing?" he asked. He couldn't look at Olivia without crying. And what would he tell the children? How could he look them in the eyes and tell them that he was unfaithful to their mother? When I met with David, he said that he didn't deserve the forgiveness of Olivia or his children. From his perspective, his future was hopeless, and he would lose his family forever.

After a few days, Olivia made her decision. She wanted to walk through the restoration process with David. Upon hearing this, David experienced a sense of relief. His eyes could see a light of hope at the end of his tunnel of despair. He said that he was willing to do anything it would take to win Olivia back. Olivia expressed a deep desire to forgive him, but she struggled with trust. How could she trust him after he betrayed her like this? Although the process of restoration would be difficult, both proclaimed they were willing to commit to it.

We met together for several weeks. My office echoed with shouts of anger, sighs of relief, weeping, laughter, the reading of Scripture and prayers. Some days were good days. Other days were more difficult. Through hard work, truth, grace and commitment, Olivia was able to forgive David. She was also able to give him practical steps toward rebuilding her trust. Each day, David was faithful to the steps Olivia gave him. And her level of trust in him began to grow.

With their marriage restored, Olivia and David began to examine the relational walls that led to the affair. Since their pain was healed, they could examine the overall history of their marriage. Both highlighted dissatisfactions they carried prior to the affair. Through Christ, they overcame each one. They worked through their differences and learned to walk together as one flesh. Their children were able to witness the power of Jesus Christ's grace and truth through their parents. David and Olivia are a walking testimony that Christ's grace can overcome any marriage crisis.

What was the turning point for David and Olivia? What set them apart from so many other couples who experience a crisis in marriage? How did they overcome the painful affair? The turning point for David and Olivia occurred before they began walking through the restoration process. It actually began when they crossed a crucial line in their minds. When Olivia and David chose to work on their marriage, their feet left the path leading to divorce. Instead of throwing in the towel of defeat, they chose to follow God's design. That simple choice altered the course of their marriage and family. Before they experienced restoration, they made a cognitive choice to move in that direction.

David and Olivia's story reminds me that it is never too late to return to God's design for marriage. It is NEVER too late! I believe this truth with all of my heart. Why? My eyes have witnessed countless stories like David and Olivia's unfold. Our God is a God of restoration. No matter what you've said or done, you are only one decision away from the good. And that good is to embrace God's design for oneness.

When We Fail...

I cannot count the number of times that I've dropped the ball as a husband. All it takes is one selfish decision to enter the Insanity Cycle. If I had a dollar for every second that Melissa and I stepped into the Insanity Cycle, my bank account would be overflowing! Recognizing the Insanity Cycle as early as possible is best.

When we fall into sin, it is easy to get down on ourselves. We feel like failures. Sometimes it seems like we will never get things right. Have you been there? When is the last time you spent a day in the Insanity Cycle? Perhaps you have been living in the Insanity Cycle for so long, that you struggle to remember when you entered it. What did you say or do to get you there? Remember that James 3:2 says, *"We all stumble in many ways."* This truth is much easier to stomach when you aren't preparing an apology sandwich for your spouse.

Most husbands and wives have specific sins they struggle with. There are days when it seems like we cannot break free from these sins. Temptation feels too big to overcome. It is much easier to move past a sin that doesn't fall into this category. But when we continually commit the same sin over and over, we experience a sense of defeat. *Why did I do that again? I cannot believe it! Last week, I asked for God and my spouse to forgive me. And I promised them that I wouldn't do this again. And here I am! I cannot ask for their forgiveness again. This time, I've sinned one too many times. I need to prove that I'm sorry first. After I do better, then I will confess the sin and get forgiveness.* Does this thought pattern sound familiar to you?

God's perspective is much different from ours. 2 Chronicles 7:14 says, *"If my people, who are called by*

my name, will humble themselves and pray and seek my
face and turn from their wicked ways, then I will hear
from heaven and will forgive their sin and will heal their
land." This verse is packed with hope! It promises that
forgiveness and healing are within our grasp. Why
would God include verses like this in Scripture? He
knows our tendency to rebel against Him! He also
understands that failure may prevent us from seeking His
forgiveness. So He included verses like 2 Chronicles
7:14 to provide an open door to reconciliation with Him.

Do you need to walk through God's open door of
reconciliation? Have you and your spouse been camping
out in the Insanity Cycle? The Insanity Cycle is a terrible
place to live. It is packed with pain, frustration and
confusion. Aren't you tired of trying to earn forgiveness?
Aren't you tired of settling for second best in your
marriage?

Let me offer you a word of encouragement. You do
not have to live there! God's grace is sufficient for your
marriage. Follow these steps provided in 2 Chronicles
7:14. By doing so, your marriage will be refreshed by
the healing that comes from forgiveness.

1. Humble yourself. Recognize the fact that you cannot
experience God's best without Him. You will never
become the husband or wife that your spouse needs by

your own power. Acknowledge the fact that you need God's help!

2. Seek God's face through prayer. Confess your sins to God and your spouse. Bring each sin into the light. Accept the grace of Jesus Christ. And forgive one another. When we confess our sins to Christ, He will forgive us. When we confess the sins we have committed against our spouse, we will open the door for healing to take place.

3. Take responsibility for yourself. Turn away from sinful behaviors that have hindered oneness in your marriage. Don't make excuses for yourself. And stop pointing fingers at the shortcomings of your spouse. Focus on your own shortcomings. Which of your behaviors are unloving or disrespectful? Repent from these destructive behaviors and submit to God's design. Husbands, cherish your wife! Wives, respect your husband!

Our God is the God of restoration. He is not a tyrant in the sky. He is not sitting on a cloud, waiting for you to mess up so that He can zap you with a lightening bolt. God does not want to destroy you. He wants to empower you to be the best spouse you can be. God loves you and wants you to succeed. He wants your marriage to experience His absolute best!

The next time you stumble into the Insanity Cycle, do not stay there. The Insanity Cycle is Satan's playground. Our minds can be filled with all kinds of negative thoughts. *I'm a failure! My spouse deserves better. I will never get this thing called marriage right.* Don't believe those lies. For we have a God of restoration. He is bigger than your worst case scenario. Your difficulty may seem like a mountain, standing between you and your spouse. Trust in God's power. He wants to move those mountains! Stop believing the negative thoughts in your mind. Look to the heavens and open your ears to God's desire for you. Listen carefully. He's cheering you on.

"The LORD your God is with you. He is mighty to save. He will take great delight in you. He will quiet you with His love. He will rejoice over you with singing."
- Zephaniah 3:17

Acknowledgements

This book came from the hearts of many friends and family. I love you all! Thank You for playing a vital role in starting the One Flesh Revolution.

My Wife & Best Friend, Melissa- Thank You for always believing in me! By the side of every great man is a Go-God-Rocking-Awesome wife. I love You deeper than deep.

My Dad and Mom, Joe & Mickie Widner- Thank You for introducing me to Christ and teaching me to chase after Him. You are an ongoing fountain of wisdom.

Darryl & Kara Bellar - Many thanks to you, my Friends. Thank You for inviting me on the adventure of a lifetime. Thank You for reminding me that the Church is the hope of the world. Thank You for showing me what the Church can be like...when God's people walk in His grace and truth. The Church in Acts is alive and well!

Greg & Carrie Beavers- Thank You for being crazy enough to believe that Christ wants to use ordinary people like us for an extraordinary mission. God placed the One Flesh Revolution in our hearts. Together, we will show the multitudes how to walk in oneness!

Ben Hall, Rick Lee, Jonathan Mock & the Journey Staff- Our eyes have seen and our ears have heard what Christ is doing through the Journey Church. Thank You for modeling what it means to follow Jesus.

My Faith Family at the Journey Church - Thank You for your love and affirmation. Your passion to obey Jesus Christ inspires me.

Brandon Harless- Thank You for designing the One Flesh logo, book cover and book format. Your creative skills are much appreciated. I owe you lots of Brother Bucks!

Jennifer Jones - Thank You for the hours you invested in editing this book! Your input has been extremely helpful.

Brandon Beavers - Thank you for providing the great picture for the back of the book!

Robert Lewis, Founder of Men's Fraternity- Thank You for giving me permission to use some of the common manhood wounds from Men's Fraternity & 33 Series.

For You The Reader- Thank You for purchasing this book. I hope my words encourage you. If so, may it remind you that God loves to use ordinary people for His extraordinary purposes. May Christ's ways shine brightly through us.

A special thanks goes out to the following people who faithfully served on the One Flesh Revolution Book Launch Team. You sacrificed your time and money to help husbands and wives. Thank You!!!

Greg & Carrie Beavers

Beth Broshears

Shawn & Ashley Buis

Daniel & Kerry Byrd

Peter & Amy Cain

Billy & Jenni Clark

Bill & Krista Comai

Michelle & Bob Corley

Adam & Sonya Crain

Julian & Shirley Culvern

Michael & Amy Edmunds

Shaun & Kacie Forbes

Justin & Mollie Garrett

CB & Maria Gerick

Greg & Julia Grant

Billy & Patricia Guin

Ben & Heather Hall

Phil & Tammy Harless

Brandon Harless

Ken & Marti Hicks

Eric & Franca Higginbotham

Jeph & Kayla Hurst

Caleb & LeLyne Joyner

Rick & Linda Keck

Rick Lee &
Sheryl
Longobardo

Paul and Brooke
Magnuson

Matt & Cassie
McCook

Charlie & Stacy
McDonough

Mitch & Dede
Mitchell

Jonathan &
Elisha Mock

David & Alyson
Neilson

Joel & Heather
Owen

Phillip &
Michelle Parker

Chuck & Dana
Peterman

Jarrett & Amy
Potts

David &
Brittany Pritchett

Tom & Karen
Ray

John & Debbie
Reed

Robert Ricker

Bryan & Kim
Simpkins

Tommy & Kathy
Snapp

Jason & Casey
Summey

Michael & Sue
Turner

Richard &
Madalyn White

Joe & Mickie
Widner

Clint & Ashley
Wilder

Michael &
Ashley Williams

David & Lisa
Williamson

Michelle Wrye

About The Author

Seth Widner is the husband of Melissa and the daddy of Judah. He serves as the Family Pastor of the Journey Church in Fernandina Beach, Florida. (www.thejourneyfamily.com) He has been able to witness God grow the Journey from a handful of faithful members to over 1,000 in attendance weekly. Go God!

Seth graduated from Johnson University in Knoxville, TN, and has been serving families in ministry for over 16 years. Seth is also a Certified Life Coach through CoachNet International. He is thankful for the opportunity to witness God move mountains in the hearts of husbands and wives.

Seth & Melissa are also cofounders of The One Flesh Revolution. The One Flesh Revolution offers marriage conferences for couples to refuel their passion for marriage. If you would like more information on upcoming conferences or would like to schedule one, please email onefleshrevolution@gmail.com.

Like One Flesh Revolution on Facebook and follow Seth on Twitter @thesethwidner

16803432R10115

Made in the USA
Charleston, SC
11 January 2013